How to
FRANCHISE
Your **Successful**
BUSINESS

A **4-Phase Guide** to BUSINESS EXPANSION

JASON R. ANDERSON, MBA

Foreword by **RAY TITUS**
CEO, UNITED FRANCHISE GROUP

How to Franchise Your Successful Business: A 4-Phase Guide to Business Expansion
By Jason R. Anderson, MBA

1. Business & Economics : Franchises
2. Business & Economics : Small Business
3. Business & Economics : New Business Enterprises

ISBN (paperback)   978-1-7352656-0-5
ISBN (ebook)   978-1-7352656-1-2

Library of Congress Control Number: 2020913239

Edited by Tamma Ford
Proofreading by Jeffrey Cleek
Book design by DTPerfect.com

Published by Franchise Consulting Group
Dallas, TX

Contact the author at **www.HowToFranchiseBook.com**

Get the most out of your franchising journey

This book comes with a companion workbook, videos, and additional resources. All are available at

www.HowToFranchiseBook.com

CONTENTS

Foreword

by **Ray Titus,**
CEO, United Franchise Group

In 2020 franchising represents 785,000+ businesses and 8.6M employees with a $500B impact on the American GDP alone. According to Darrell Johnson, CEO of FRANdata, "Without a doubt, franchising plays a major role in our economy and we forecast that most franchise businesses will sustain robust growth in 2020."

As the CEO of United Franchise Group, I consistently promote to our employees and Franchisees alike the need to read! This is a step by step franchising book that is a must-read for anyone thinking about franchising their business.

Jason started with UFG as a Regional Vice President for our Transworld brand, and over the years has moved up to become President of Venture X, the CNBC ranked fastest growing Flexible Office Space provider in the country. We've grown the concept from one single location in Naples, FL in 2016 to 32 locations open and 125 sold in 31 countries in only 4 years. With an average investment of $2M+ per location, this was no small feat. His knowledge of the "in's" and "out's" of franchising is very apparent.

The book talks about the four key areas: Strategic Planning, Legal Documentation, Franchise Operations, and Sales/Franchisee Support. These are a great, practical way to start your franchise company, and Jason's examples and stories help anyone understand the steps needed to franchise. I have been in franchising for 34 years and we currently have 10 brands with over 1600 franchisees in 70+ countries. Jason has taken some of what we do and condensed it into this step by step guide. After reading this book, and apply-ing its principles, I have no doubt you and your company will be in a much better place to succeed in franchising.

Thank you, Jason, and good luck to you and the readers in building the next Great Franchise Co.

What This Book Will Show You

This book is an in-depth look at everything you need to know on How to Franchise Your Business with as little of a sales pitch as possible (Disclaimer: I do operate as a franchising consultant — obviously — and would be more than happy to work with you). In these pages, you will learn about your path to successfully franchising your business:

- What exactly is franchising?

- Why franchise?

- How much will franchising my business cost?

- How long will franchising my business take?

- How many locations do I need to have before franchising my business?

- Franchising vs licensing and other growth options

- Franchising laws, rules, and regulations

- The four phases to franchising your business

All the available options for franchising your business are clearly outlined — including DIY, working with a consultant, working with an attorney, or completely outsourcing the franchising of your business. There are a few good books on the topic, but none of them really include the nuts and bolts of how to actually put your franchise together. Like almost everything in life, it is possible to completely franchise your business on your own. But it's also possible to build your own house, car, or airplane. However, most people clearly understand that with no experience those things are not good ideas.

So if I don't recommend doing it 100% on your own, why write a book on How to Franchise Your Business? The answer is simple — because I will always recommend that you study and understand the first 80% on your own before you even consider spending $1 with a consultant or attorney to discuss franchising your business.

Many of my clients realize after going through this process that franchising is the least risky, lowest cost method for dramatically expanding their business. Some owners even realize that franchising is the only viable method of expansion for their type of business. Most importantly, there will be those business owners who go through this book and realize that franchising is not right for them.

Most business owners do not realize that franchising already dominates every industry it is involved in. From fast food, sports bars, hotels, gas stations, car washes, pack & ship, barbershops, massage parlors, gyms, janitorial services, residential real estate, car dealerships, painting, lawn maintenance and even pet poop clean-up services…basically every industry is touched by franchising.

Through this book and every step of franchising, you will be able to determine if this is the right method for you to grow your business. The cost associated with franchising your business is not as high as you might think, and typically involves a significantly lower money amount and risk than opening another location on your own. Most importantly, you will learn what to do after you have franchised your business.

PART ONE

Understanding the Concept of Franchising

JUST WHAT IS FRANCHISING?

Franchises are found on virtually every corner of our cities, in every sector of our economy. Each one started with a standalone business that worked and made money for its owners. Each franchise began when those owners wanted a way to grow their business and adding numerous new 'corporate-owned' locations across the nation or around the world was not the way they wanted to achieve it.

In layman's terms, franchising is packaging your business processes — its marketing, branding, systems, services, products, and location 'look' — and then teaching someone else how to clone it for an upfront fee (Franchise Fee) and charging an ongoing fee for the support that you provide (Royalty).

In the relationship, you as the original business owner are called the Franchisor, and the person you sell the business model to is your Franchisee. The business location that the franchisee owns and operates is commonly called the franchise. The document that you must provide the potential franchisee is the Franchise Disclosure Document (or FDD) and the agreement you sign with a confirmed franchisee is the Franchise Agreement (or FA). Franchising in the United States is regulated; the Federal Trade Commission (FTC) is the regulatory agency.

That is a lot of information straight out of the gate, I know. But these are the foundational terms you need to understand before any of this will make sense. I've spent hours on calls with people, and then spoken to them a few days later or via email and they refer to themselves as the wrong person in the relationship.

Many business models and industries are already dominated by franchising. Franchising is not just for fast food restaurants, as many people think. When most people read the Entrepreneur Franchise 500 list for the first time, they are surprised at how many different industries and companies are dominated by franchising.

For many business types, franchising may be the only logical way to grow your business. Franchising (when done right) may also be the lowest risk, require the lowest upfront capital, and have the best potential to lead to amazing growth for you, your brand, and your franchisees.

The list below is a demonstration that virtually every industry is touched by franchising. I compiled the list below by going through the top 100 of the Franchise 500 and selecting 50 of those 100 that were in different industries.

You see the range of industries and activities that franchising has treated very well:

- Dunkin = Fast Casual Coffee & Donuts
- McDonald's = Burgers
- The UPS Store = Mail, Ship & Delivery
- Ace Hardware = Hardware Store
- Planet Fitness = Gym
- Jersey Mike's = Subs
- Pizza Hut = Pizza
- 7-Eleven = Gas & Retail
- Kumon Math & Reading = Tutoring
- Baskin Robbins = Ice Cream
- Budget Blinds = Blinds
- HomeVestors/We Buy Ugly Homes = Real Estate Investing
- Palm Beach Tan = Tanning
- uBreakiFix = Cell Phone Repair
- KFC = Chicken
- SuperCuts = Haircuts
- ServPro = Disaster Recovery
- Goldfish Swim School = Swimming Lessons
- Mathnasium = Tutoring
- Hampton Inn = Hotel
- Snap-on Tools = Tools
- Fyzical Therapy = Physical Therapy
- Jan-Pro = Janitorial Service
- Remax = Residential Real Estate
- Nothing Bundt Cakes = Dessert
- Cruise Planners = Cruises
- Pet Supplies Plus = Pet Supplies
- Express Employment = Staffing
- Lawn Doctor = Lawn Care
- Primrose School = Daycare
- FastSigns = Signs
- European Wax Center = Waxing

- Valvoline Instant Oil Change = Oil Change
- Pearle Vision = Eyecare
- Kona Ice = Shaved Ice
- Profile by Sanford = Weight loss
- Club Pilates = Pilates
- Dogtopia = Dog Boarding
- Dream Vacations = Vacation Planning
- Chem-Dry = Carpet Cleaning
- Sola Salon Studios = Salon Suites
- The Joint = Chiropractor
- Urban Air Adventure Park = Trampoline Park
- ASP America's Swimming Pool = Pool Maintenance
- Rooter Man = Drain Cleaning
- Fleet Feet = Running Shoes
- Big O Tires = Tires
- Drybar = Hair Salon
- Tide Cleaners = Dry Cleaners
- Miracle Ear = Hearing Aid

(Source: *41st Annual 2020 Entrepreneur Franchise 500 Rankings,* https://www.entrepreneur.com/franchise500/2020)

As you can see, just in the first 100 of the 500 franchises there are already 50 distinct industries, and even more if you count the different types of foods represented. This shows you that essentially any business model can be franchised successfully. I especially like to point out the dog poop clean-up franchises when I discuss this. Yes — dog poop. There are three major players that claim to be #1 in this business when it comes to pets:

- Pet Butler (https://www.petbutler.com)
- Doody Calls (https://doodycalls.com)
- Poop 911 (https://www.poop911.com)

If that doesn't get you to buy into the fact that your business may also be franchiseable — then nothing will! You might as well save yourself some time and stop reading this book right now! Franchising must be a win-win scenario for it to grow for you as the franchisor and for the person you sell your franchise to, the franchisee:

- As the franchisor, you must receive a benefit for all the hard work and effort that has gone into making your business successful, and your capacity to teach that to someone else.

- As a franchisee, you want to ensure that you receive not only a positive return on your investment, but a higher quality of life and a bigger sense of purpose than you had in your salaried or prior job.

Let's review the 'easy' terminology.

- You, the founder, are called "The Franchisor" and the person you sell the opportunity to is called your "Franchisee".

- The upfront fee they pay you to have the right to open a location within your franchise is called a "Franchise Fee". Franchise Fees might range anywhere from $5,000 to $80,000, but the average is $20,000 to $35,000.

- The ongoing fee they pay, often annually, is called a "Royalty". Royalties can be presented as a monthly flat fee or as a percentage, and I have seen one that was 25%.

- The FDD, or Franchise Disclosure Document, is not a contract but tells prospective franchisees all about you and the opportunity, with no obligation on either side.

- The FA, or Franchise Agreement, is a legally binding contract between one franchisor (you) and one franchisee to do business together.

It's also important to note that you create those numbers depending on your specific business model. Your franchise fee and royalty could be zero or $100,000, or even more if you want it to be. However, this book will help you find what's common in your industry, and how to ensure that you are competitive to prospective franchisees.

To help expand your understanding of the concept, here are other definitions of franchising:

Wikipedia: https://en.wikipedia.org/wiki/Franchising

"Franchising is based on a marketing concept which can be adopted by an organization as a strategy for business expansion. Where implemented, a franchisor licenses its know-how, procedures, intellectual property, use of its business model, brand, and rights to sell its branded products and services to a franchisee. In return the franchisee pays certain fees and agrees to comply with certain obligations, typically set out in a Franchise Agreement."

Entrepreneur.com: https://www.entrepreneur.com/encyclopedia/franchising

"Definition: A continuing relationship in which a franchisor provides a licensed privilege to the franchisee to do business and offers assistance in organizing, training, merchandising, marketing, and managing in return for a monetary consideration. Franchising is a form of business by which the owner (franchisor) of a product, service or method obtains distribution through affiliated dealers (franchisees)."

International Franchise Association: https://www.franchise.org/faqs/basics/what-is-a-franchise

"Franchising is a method of distributing products or services. At least two levels of people are involved in a franchise system: (1) the franchisor, who establishes the brand's trademark or trade name and a business system; and (2) the franchisee, who pays a royalty and often an initial fee for the right to do business under the franchisor's name and system. Technically, the contract binding the two parties is the 'franchise,' but that term is often used to mean the actual business that the franchisee operates."

I hope those words help you understand the general concept of franchising. Again: you as the business owner/founder are the "Franchisor"; the person you sell to is the "Franchisee"; the process of the model is what we call "Franchising". The upfront fee you collect is called the "Franchise Fee"; the ongoing or recurring fee is your "Royalty". The document that you must provide the potential franchisee is the "Franchise Disclosure Document"; the agreement they sign is the "Franchise Agreement".

This all sounds very exciting, and there are many compelling reasons for entering the world of franchising. But before we go any further, I want to outline why I'm uniquely qualified to take you on this franchising journey, and why it has been such a big part of my life.

MY FRANCHISING JOURNEY

Over the last eight years I've helped hundreds of business owners like yourself take their business to the next level by franchising. And before that, I built the 8th largest residential real estate brokerage by transaction volume in the State of Texas.

I have been blessed to be featured on the cover of *Realtor Magazine*, to win the *Dallas Business Journal* Minority Business Leader Award, and to be featured on TLC's *My First Home*. But my proudest achievement was being nominated in the first edition of the *Forbes* 30 Under 30 in 2012. Today, I'm the president of Venture X (https://venturex.com/) — the fastest growing co-working space franchise in the world, with 30+ locations open, and 120+ sold in 30 countries.

I also know the struggle and tenacity it takes to thrive and even survive during tough times. As the youngest of 10 and having joined the United States Air Force at 17 years of age, I had my general struggles in life as a young man. I joined the military during the summer of 2000, and about 15 months later the planes hit the towers on 9/11. I was 18 years old at the time, on active duty, and stationed in the United Kingdom. This tragedy ultimately led to me starting my own business on base, which then supported me after leaving the military.

Then I experienced another major problem. Back in the summer of 2007, I decided to get my real estate license. I did so and launched my own new real estate business. Then a few months later, The Great Recession hit. But again, it was a blessing in disguise and led to me taking on a unique opportunity at a unique time in history. I was not alone in launching during this downturn. A few other small companies that you might have heard about started during the Great Recession:

- Credit Karma
- WhatsApp (sold for $19B)
- Venmo
- Groupon
- Instagram
- Uber
- Pinterest
- Slack
- Square

I've heard people say that it was just a sign of the times, and these companies launching between 2007 to 2010 was a fluke. So I looked back to all the companies that I could find that started during recessions for the last 120 years. I was surprised to find the following:

- GM = 1907 Recession
- HP = 1939 (The Great Depression & WWII)

- Burger King (Franchise) = 1950's (Korean War Depression)

- Hyatt (franchise) = 1950's (Korean War Depression)

- Trader Joe's = 1950's (Korean War Depression)

- Microsoft = 1975 (Oil Embargo Recession)

- CNN = 1980's (Inflation Rate Recession)

- Electronic Arts (EA) = 1980's Global Energy Crisis

I'm finishing this book as America is now several months into Covid-19, with all its economic and social ramifications. But I'm still going strong. My business is still selling franchises.

As you can see, there is no excuse for waiting. The timing has never been — and it never will be — better to take your current business to the next level via franchising. Now more than ever, people are looking for structured business opportunities they can invest in, from which they will acquire a sense of ownership and pride, and consequently build a better future for themselves and their families.

SO HOW DID I GET INTO FRANCHISING?

My journey began 10 years ago. Just like many of you, I was a successful small business owner looking to expand my business. I decided to look at case studies for the three largest competitors in my space. (I recommend, before we get started, you take a few seconds and think about your own top 3 competitors, and study up on what they have been doing over time).

I was running a residential real estate company in Dallas, Texas, that I grew from zero to over 200 agents in 4 years with 3 offices. I was blessed to win those awards I mentioned as an outcome of this success.

Even with all those awards, I could not wrap my head around a way to go from my three locations and 200 agents to 900+ offices with 180,000 agents like Keller Williams…or to 6800 offices in 100 countries with 100,000+ agents like Remax…or to 9400 offices with 127,000+ agents like Century 21. I simply couldn't comprehend how they were able to accomplish these goals. Then through some basic research I found out the one main thing they all had in common was FRANCHISING. I sold my real estate company to a publicly traded corporation and headed into the world of franchises.

I was lucky to find and work with one of the largest privately owned franchise companies in the country. Over the last 8 years, I've learned a lot about franchising from the ground up by doing it every day and helping to grow franchise brands. In 2018, I wrote a book called *How to Franchise Your Business* that sold copies worldwide. I've taught Franchising 101 (not the real name of the classes) at the college level and have spoken at dozens of events. I've worked with companies of all sizes, in every industry from dog poop cleaning (seriously), to food, retail, service, tax, eye lashes, and massage.

I have also turned down hundreds of companies over the years that had great business models. For one or many reasons, franchising was just not a good fit for them. There are mainly four reasons for turning down so many clients after the initial franchise feasibility study, and these include:

- Lack of capital (fancy way of saying they were broke or not yet profitable)

- Lack of operations systems and processes (fancy way of saying they did not have their sh*t together or were just doing things by the seat of their pants)

- No competitive advantage (from a consumer's point of view)

- Not a replicable business model

- Extra Bonus Reason = The business was illegal

Also, it is important to note here that after attending three months of law school prep courses, I dropped out of the program. So I am not in any way, shape, or form an attorney — and I do not pretend to be. Everything in this book is from my personal experience and should not be taken as legal advice. Whenever legal questions arise as you prepare to become a franchisor, please consult a reputable, franchise-savvy attorney. It will be worth the investment.

So now you know who I am and some of the benefits of franchising, you're ready to move onto Chapter 1, which helps you determine if franchising is right for your business.

Why Franchising?

By far the number one reason business owners franchise is that they realize — or better yet, their customers realize — that they have a great business model, and that effective business model should also be migrated to other cities, states, and countries.

The Top Scenario Leading to Franchise

Growth. You want to expand your business.

You know, however, that you do not have the time and/or money to grow. The problem is you are already working 60+ hours a week to make a living (or to make ends meet) and do not have the money and/or time to expand to more locations on your own. Franchising for most is the lowest-cost way to expand.

Let's say you own an independent retail or fast casual business that cost you $250,000 to open from scratch. Or you own a home-based business that cost $50,000 to open from scratch. Now let's say your dream is to have 10 more locations open.

- For the retail business that's $250,000 x 10 = $2,500,000. You will need $2,500,000 to open 10 new locations.

- For the home-based business, you will need $500,000 using the same math.

Those numbers don't include ongoing employee payrolls, rent, insurance, liabilities, and the struggle of managing 10 locations on your own. You can easily see why almost no business does it this way.

If you plan on (or dream of) expanding your business, there are only a few options available to grow.

- DIY, Do it at all yourself. You have:
  - 100% of the work
  - 100% risk
  - 100% reward
- Take on Partners or Investors. You have:
  - 100% of the work
  - a shared risk and reward

The Second Scenario

You have the money, but don't have the time.

I've met dozens of successful entrepreneurs — some of whom have indeed opened as many as 10 locations on their own. They come to realize that managing and being responsible for multiple locations is simply an unmanageable task from a time perspective.

We've helped those owners turn their businesses into franchises, and then sell their existing locations to Franchisees for a Franchise Fee. The owners who are now Franchisors collect periodic royalties after the sales. You can perhaps picture a successful franchisor now, with a Corona in hand at a luxury ocean front villa, wondering "Why didn't I do this sooner?"

The Third Reason

It's what all your top competitors have done to grow.

In many cases, following the masses is a bad idea, but if you are the type who is still making mixtapes on your CD burner, or using your good ole trusty flip phone, then franchising may not be for you.

On a more serious note, franchising may be your best and, in many cases, your only option for growth, if that's what most of your competition has done to expand their reach. As an example, if you own a fast-casual food concept, basically every major national player is a franchise, publicly traded company, or both. The same applies for residential real estate brokerages (like my scenario), janitorial services, and almost all home service companies.

A Fourth Scenario

You want to grow outside of your own area or town.

This is an easy one to explain. If your business is in Charlotte, North Carolina, and you want to open a location in Dallas, Texas, how do you achieve that? Would you rather pay all the opening costs, take on the liability, and then hire a stranger to run your business 1025.80 miles away (yes, Google it; you cannot drive that far and back again, even once monthly)? Or would you rather have someone pay you and take on the risk and cost to open your same business in Dallas? That is why franchising is so powerful — it makes long-distance expansion possible.

The Fifth Reason

You're a "give me a small piece of a bigger pie" type of person.

I've worked with all types of entrepreneurs and not all of them would make good franchisors for many reasons. But the main one is that they — from their personal mindset — would prefer to have "a big piece of a smaller pie" vs "a small piece of a bigger pie" type of business. There are billionaire franchisors, such as:

- Michael Ilitch from Little Caesars
- Jack Taylor from Enterprise Rent-A-Car
- William Hilton & John Marriot (hints in the names)
- the late Fred DeLuca of Subway
- Jimmy John Liautaud of Jimmy John's Gourmet Sandwiches

Case in point: As of last year, 2019, the founder of Jimmy John's has a net worth of $1.7B, by earning a 6% royalty from the roughly 3000 franchisees.

None of these were overnight billionaires. They were sure smart ones, though.

(Source: https://www.forbes.com/sites/giacomotognini/2019/09/25/inspire-brands-expands-its-restaurant-empire-purchasing-jimmy-johns-at-undisclosed-price/#33848e5c4192)

5 REASONS YOU SHOULD *NOT* FRANCHISE YOUR BUSINESS

Let's be clear about why you should not choose franchising for your business. Again, I see five scenarios or reasons not to go this route.

My Top Reason for Not Franchising

Your business is not yet profitable!

This may sound like a no-brainer, but I've had many people reach out, with the view that franchising is a way of raising capital to grow their business. That is the opposite of what franchising was intended for. If your business is not turning a profit, no investor or entrepreneur in their right mind (many people are not in their right mind!) would buy it. You need to be making money and be profitable, consistently, if you are looking to franchise.

An easy way to determine if your business profit is substantial enough to consider franchising is by looking at your P&L. Take 6% (for a typical business this can be any percentage that you choose) off the top line revenue and see what that does to your bottom line.

- For a business with $1M top line revenue with a 15% net profit of $150,000. If you take 6% of $1M that's $60,000 and subtract that from $150,000. You are left with $90,000 profit for the franchisee. That's a business that could make sense to franchise.

- I've had a food concept that required 15 to 20 employees and had $500K top line revenue and 10% net profit or $50,000 profit. If you take 6% from $500,000 that's $30,000 and subtract that from

$50,000, you're only left with $20,000 profit to the franchisee. That business is not well-placed to franchise.

The Number Two Reason for Not Franchising

You can't logically answer the "why" question!

If a prospect asks you, "Why would I buy your concept over [insert your top franchise competitor name]?" and you don't have a logical answer, you are dead in the water. You need to have a good pitch, followed by logical reasoning as to why someone would buy your new, higher risk concept over the other already-established player. 2-3 simple statements are fine (you don't need an entire PowerPoint presentation); a simple 60-second elevator pitch can do the trick. Your answer to "Why you?" could be lower cost, higher quality, increasing (high-level of steady) demand, technology efficiencies, more profit…

A Third Don't-Do-It Scenario

You are looking to get rich quick!

This sounds cliché, but many of the clients I've talked with are looking for an easy way to make more money on their existing business. While this is possible after years of hard work (see the above list of billionaire franchisors), this should not be your primary reason for franchising. In a later section, we will see that the work you do on financial modelling helps determine how much money you could make from franchising your business.

Don't be fooled: Franchising in the first few years will be as much work as opening a location on your own, if not more. But the long-term goal is for you to not be involved in daily operations at all of those many locations (if that's what you choose).

A Fourth Reason to Stay Away from Franchising

You're a control freak and believe no one knows better than you.

I've seen many business owners look to expand via franchising and/or partnerships, yet each time they try, it crumbles. At some point, you have to realize that you're the common denominator in the failure. Only you can recognize this.

Connected to control, it may also be true that your business cannot exist without you, and that your special skills are what make it unique. This is true for many medical professions, or industries that require high levels of certification, regulation, unique experience, or technical skills.

The Last of Five Reasons Not to Franchise

Your industry as a whole is not really suitable for franchising.

For example, I had a client who was a CPA and wanted to franchise. We found out late into the process that CPA firms, with their heavy regulatory environment, are not suitable for franchising. Likewise, most online non-service related businesses don't make sense for franchising.

Also in this unsuitable-for-franchising category are illegal businesses. A retired teacher that started a home-based mobile delivery bakery was making 6 figures. It was a great concept, but franchising was instantly eliminated because it is illegal to run food businesses out of your home in most states.

Single product-based concepts without a service concept behind them are also unsuitable for franchising. Maybe you've invented the next Pet Rock or Beanie Baby — that could be a great product (seasonal; while the trend lasts; etc.), but not a good franchise opportunity for someone.

SOME REAL ISSUES YOU SHOULD ALSO CONSIDER

Some of the five reasons to franchise and five reasons not to franchise may have resonated with you. Let's walk through some additional issues to see if you are ready to move into franchising or not.

Issue: Personal capacity. You are looking to expand and you're considering opening another location. One of the quickest tests (it is more art than science to see if you are financially ready to franchise) is to determine if you have the capacity mentally, physically, and financially to open another location. In the early days of a franchisor's life — i.e., during the launch of the first ten franchisees — it's going to require about the same amount of time, energy, and effort you would initially have in opening a location on your own. The difference is you are not paying the bills, signing the lease, and managing the employees. But you should still expect to invest close to about what it would cost you to open another location of your own, as you build your franchise company.

As an example, a brand new (done right) location would cost $250,000 to open. You should expect in the first few years to invest roughly the same into becoming, marketing, and developing your business as a franchise.

Issue: You do or do not have your $#!T together. You have clean and well-documented records and financials, and your business has been profitable for at least two years in a row. You have good (or great) systems and processes that you feel comfortable teaching others how to do. You have staff that are on-board for expanding, and who are helping to grow a local or national brand. If you do not, then you are not ready to be a franchisor.

Issue: Time invested for preparation. You are willing to give it at least two years of your time to get launched as a franchisor. I've worked with hundreds of franchisors and, for some reason, two years seems to be the magic number for proving out a franchise concept. The first year could easily be spent on planning, documenting, registering, and launching the concept. Most of our clients can have the first part done in six months, and then spend the next 6-9 months in franchise sales and marketing efforts to find that first franchisee. And then another 9-12 months after signature are involved with helping that franchisee get up and running. If you can get one new location open by the end of the second year, and make it through that alive (and/or happy; and/or still sane!) then franchising may be the way for you to grow.

Issue: You're okay or not with the worst-case scenario. The worst-case scenario for most companies that consider franchising is this: you go through 4-6 months of R&D, invest $10,000-50,000 and end up with a complete outline of systems, processes, technology, legal documents, and a detailed plan on how to expand your business. It may not sound like a bad scenario, and from my completely biased opinion, it is not. I've had clients go through the entire process, get everything ready to franchise and decide that they will use their own money and expand on their own. The documents and processes created for franchising could easily be (and usually are) repurposed for corporate growth and strategies.

The other worst case scenario has been this: I have gone through the whole process with prospective franchisors, and they invested a much smaller amount than they would have to open up another location that may have been doomed to fail, and as a consequence they decided to sell their business (rather than expand it as previously planned). In this scenario, they were legally a franchisor with documented processes, clean books, training, and Operations Manuals. Their business became more valuable as a franchisor with zero franchisees than it would have been as a standalone, independent location, without all of the documented systems and processes.

The Many Ways to Grow Your Business

Over the years of building, buying, selling, and franchising hundreds of companies, I've realized a universal truth: There are only a handful of ways to grow and expand a business, regardless of the industry you are in.

In this chapter, we highlight the main growth methods. I have created a cheat sheet table below to compare and contrast five of them for you.

You might grow your business in these ways, or combine some of them to suit your business better:

- Organic: internally-driven growth that you mastermind yourself

- Partners: bringing in more resources and new markets, sharing risk

- Investors: for more capital to finance your internally-managed move into new markets

- Licensing: letting a manufacturer/distributor sell some/all of your products/services to a wider market than you can reach

- Franchising: read this book for how that works

- External growth: you buy other related solid companies as sole new owner and merge them into your own (seamlessly or as new divisions of your business)

- Take your business public: list it on the stock exchange

Perhaps you find other ways to grow; chances are they incorporate one or more of the methods in the list.

For this chart below we are going to show the how a fast casual restaurant owner might approach the first 5 methods of growth:

- Fast Casual Restaurant with $300,000 startup cost

- Each location requiring 10 employees and a manager

- Partners & Investors are 50%

- Partner & Investor could be used combined for going public

	On Your Own	Partner	Investors	Licensing	Franchising
Risk	100%	50%	50%	50%	50%
Reward	100%	50%	50%	Flat Fee	5-10%
Control	100%	50%	50%	20%	100%
Natl/Intl	Very Tough	Very Tough	Tough	Possible	Logical
Cost	$$$$$	$$$$$	$$$$$	$$$	$$
Time	Extensive	Extensive	Extensive	Low	Low
Employees	All	All	All	None	None
Lease/Rent	Yes	Yes	Yes	No	No
Scalability	Low	Low	Low	Mid	High
Speed	Slow	Slow	Slow	Slow	Fast
Upfront Fee	No	No	No	Yes	Yes
Royalty	No	No	No	No	Yes
Exit Strategy	Low	Low	Low	Mid	High

- **Risk** = What percentage you as the owner have in this growth model. To even the score we set anything that involved a 2nd party (i.e. partner, investor, licensee, and franchisee) as 50%, to show that there is someone else involved.

- **Reward** = On average, the percentage of location revenue you should expect to receive

- **Control** = Who makes the decisions on the business model to the end user

- **National/International** = Capacity to grow beyond your local market including international

- **Cost** = How much out of pocket it will cost you to grow

- **Time** = How much do you have to personally spend at each location

- **Employees** = How many of the employees at new locations are you responsible for

- **Lease/Rent** = Who signs the lease and pays the rent

- **Scalability** = Probability of scale and long-term growth

- **Speed** = Speed at which the business can scale

- **Upfront Fee** = Do you get a check to open a new location

- **Royalty** = Do you collect royalties on each location

- **Exit Strategy** = Saleability of the business model when you're ready

WHAT'S THE DIFFERENCE BETWEEN FRANCHISING AND LICENSING?

By far the most frequent question asked about business expansion is regarding the differences and similarities between franchising and licensing. Obviously, I am a franchising professional, so pardon me if I simplify somewhat here in describing the two approaches. My goal is to get terminologies and pros and cons across clearly. Keep in mind, there is more to know about this, and I am not going to be covering all bases in this discussion. Also keep in mind, my earlier disclaimer: I am not an attorney; an attorney would word these explanations considerably differently!

Franchising

A franchise is an extension — in the form of a cloned business unit — of an already existing business that wants to expand its number of locations (extend its market presence). A franchise typically sells a 'concept' business. It might be a food *concept* (McDonald's, Dunkin), a janitorial *concept* (Stanley Steemer, Molly Maids), a real estate *concept* (Remax), and so on through all sectors and industries.

When you purchase a franchise, as franchisee you pay fees for the right to operate a business 'concept' in the exact way the original owner (the franchisor) wants you to, and you operate and market the business in its entirety — also in the way the franchisor wants you to.

McDonald's is a famous example of an international franchise business 'concept' which franchisees operate as such — lock, stock, and barrel — to the tune of 36,000 restaurants in more than 100 countries. In other words, there are 36,000 businesses out there that are the exact clone of the original McDonald's.

Snap-on Tools (a mobile tool store concept; high quality tool sales to professionals), Pearle Vision (eye-doctor-in-a-retail-store concept, with retail prescription eyewear), Remax (stands for 'Real Estate Maximum' whose uniqueness is the 'maximum commission concept' — meaning agents keep most of their commissions while paying the broker a share of the office expenses) are three very different *concept* businesses in the franchise world.

Licensing

A license is a legal relationship where one party, the "Licensor", grants to the other party, the "Licensee", the right to use or benefit from a trademark, technology, or other legal rights. It is quite common to see any of these types of licensing arrangements:

(a) the licensor allows the licensee the limited right to use a trademark for a limited purpose. Walt Disney grants McDonald's a license for McDonald's to co-brand its McDonald's Happy Meals with a Disney trademarked character. The burger customer might be served a Coke in a Cinderella cup.

(b) a technology company, as licensor, grants a license to an individual or members of a whole company, as licensee, to use a particular technology.

Microsoft grants a license (in today's parlance, the license means you have paid your 'annual subscription') to individual users allowing them to use the Windows operating system and/or other proprietary software applications.

(c) A license where a company that owns the patent to a certain product (like a drug, a new invention, a branded clothing item, etc.) as licensor grants a license to another company, as licensee, allowing them to manufacture and sell the product that utilizes the patented formula (process, recipe, or pattern).

You see that licensing makes sense if you do not sell a concept, but a number of proprietary products. What you are doing is licensing production with one or more licensed manufacturers who forward the manufactured products to one or more licensed distributors (= sales companies for hire). Both are licensed by you to sell your products. Neither the manufacturer nor the distributor is prohibited from producing/selling other people's products. There is no retail 'concept' for the most part (no dedicated commercial location), but instead one or more products or packages of products gain a very wide distribution due to the efforts of your licensee/distributor.

Licensing of both the manufacture and the sales/distribution is quite common for inventors of gadgets and products as a way of monetizing their inventions.

Any number of 'new-design' auto parts invented and patented by a 'back-yard mechanic' inventor (the licensor) find distribution through national auto retailers like NAPA, AutoZone, and others (the licensees). The latter retailers are the sellers/distributors or licensees; the product owner or licensor receives a pre-agreed percentage of the sale price as 'royalties'.

A famous example of licensing is, again, the 'merchandising' done by Hollywood. From Mickey Mouse to Cinderella, from Marvel to DC comic characters — any merchandise (physical product, from dolls to CD disks to posters to clothing, etc.) can be manufactured and distributed under a license granted by the owner (Disney Corp, etc.).

Control

Control is a fundamental difference between franchising and licensing. The amount of control a franchisor holds over the franchisee is greater than that of a licensor over a licensee. A franchisor supplies the business model/concept and defines the number of units and the size of territory in which any given franchisee can operate.

A licensor does not dictate the processes of manufacturing or the processes of distributions — the licensees do what they know is best, on their own, to meet the requirements of their license agreement.

When you license a product, you sell the rights to use your company's products and trademarks in exchange for some predetermined amount of royalties — but do not limit the licensee's ability to sell other products. The licensor retains ownership of the intellectual property involved.

More Examples of Licensing

Did you know when you buy a pair of Calvin Klein underwear, it's not actually made by Calvin Klein? The only clothing that the Calvin Klein company manufactures itself is some of its women's lines. Every other Calvin Klein-branded garment you buy, including perfume and jeans as well as their famous underwear, are a result of a licensing agreement. The makers of these products have licensed the Calvin Klein name and logo to help sell their own products. Calvin Klein does not tell the distributors how or where or (mostly) at what price to sell their goods. That is at the distributor's discretion.

Disney's primary competitor, Warner Bros., also draws a significant amount of revenue from the intellectual properties it owns, with DC Comics providing massive toy and apparel licensing opportunities. Even the Wizarding World of Harry Potter is the result of a licensing deal. Since Warner Bros. doesn't own any theme parks, it chose to license its theme park rights to Universal Studios to capitalize on the Harry Potter intellectual property.

BENEFITS AND DRAWBACKS OF FRANCHISING

Franchisee benefits:

- Become/remain self-employed
- Mitigate the risks of business ownership by being part of a proven business with a customer base ready to buy from you
- Potentially gain a monopoly within a particular territory

- Initially invest sums that may be lower than starting a business on your own

Franchisee drawbacks:

- loss of control, since the franchisor makes a lot of the decisions for you

- profits that tend to be lower than with your independent business, due to fees and royalties

None of the above benefits or drawbacks apply to licensors or licensees, with the possible exception of risk mitigation for both. The licensee is required by agreement to sell the agreed number of units per year or quarter. The licensor has no risk of the costs of sales (they do not do any selling) or overproduction/ underproduction (that is the manufacturer's area of influence), since all those matters are now at the discretion of the licensees.

Franchisor benefits:

- expand your business for less investment than opening new locations yourself from internal funds

- you know what the business looks like when it's successful

- take advantages of economies of scale with vendors and suppliers

- pick and choose who franchises a unit from you

- control of how operations take place in franchisee units

Franchisor drawbacks:

- federal and state filings and disclosures can seem onerous

- give up some control over ongoing quality as the franchisor can never be in all the franchised units at once to monitor them

Licensees experience reduced risk because they're usually entering the marketplace with a known product (Disney character merchandise); such products usually have pre-identified markets of consumers. On the other hand, licensees might have a higher, but calculated, risk with an unknown product such as an invention by an individual unfamiliar with distribution processes — i.e., will the product find a market or not?

A license allows the licensee to use, make and sell an idea, design, name, or logo for a fee. The advantage is that there is no expense for research and development of the product. The disadvantage is that most license agreements require the distributor to sell a (usually high) minimum number of units per period, and it takes attention and skill to achieve that level of sales.

Licensor:
A licensor retains legal ownership of a licensed product. Licenses are advantageous for licensors because they allow them to expand their sales reach and brand notoriety without having to invest heavily in new locations and distribution/sales networks, additional marketing, and advertising.

LICENSING AND FRANCHISING: WHICH ONE IS RIGHT FOR YOU?

Every business has its potential challenges. As you consider the difference between franchising and licensing, add up the pros and cons of your situation, goals, personality, and products. Also, remember to consider the resources you have available when making your decision.

FRANCHISING VERSUS CORPORATE GROWTH

The first of the growth methodologies is organic or internally-generated growth. If you are torn between franchising and growing your business directly, there is good news: you can do both!

Grow your original business internally:

- hire a newly pumped-up sales team responsible for national, regional, and local territories

- add an eCommerce division to your business (I know one metaphysical merchandise retail store that built its eCommerce website to "add a bit to the bottom line"; it turned out the eCommerce website was bringing in 90% of the top line revenues within 2 years for the business).

While some of your people are achieving that internally-driven organic growth, work on franchising, too. Some businesses have about a 50/50 corporate location vs franchisee location split and that works for them. Make sure to carve out territories reserved for corporate growth and others for franchisee growth. One of our clients has reserved for themselves their entire state for corporate expansion, while another client we work with has kept only a single county for corporate expansion. There is no right or wrong answer.

Are your biggest competitors offering franchises or licensing agreements? Not that this should be the ultimate determining factor, but if most of your major competitors are doing one or the other that should be something you consider!

BACK TO FRANCHISING

Here are some questions I ask my own clients to help them decide how they really want to go about achieving business growth:

- Do you want to grow your brand name and make the buyer use your brand name?

- Do you dream of seeing your brand all over the country or the world — like McDonald's or Starbucks?

- Do you want to charge an upfront fee for selling your business concept?

- Do you want to charge people a sizeable upfront fee? Let's say anything more than $500 to pay you, for your knowledge and training on launching the business?

- Would you like to collect ongoing royalties?

- Do you want to continue to support and profit from your franchisee's growth, or do you want to just sell them a service or product and move on?

If you have answered yes to two or more of these questions, then franchising is probably the way to go for your business.

Let's take a deeper dive now into what is involved in becoming a franchisor.

The Federal Trade Commission (FTC) and The Franchise Rule

I don't want to bore you with too much legal mumbo jumbo in these pages, but it's very important for you to understand some basic legal aspects of what being a franchisor means.

I say this because the government, through the FTC (Federal Trade Commission), is involved in the franchising process. The FTC has defined what a franchise is and other aspects of franchise ownership, creation, and transmission. The FTC spells out the exact process that must be taken to become a franchisor.

After spending close to a decade helping launch hundreds of concepts as franchise organizations — and regardless of the industry, size, investment, secret sauce — I've seen that virtually all companies follow the same path or process in regard to becoming a franchisor.

Much of this similarity is because the FTC (Federal Trade Commission) is involved in how it happens.

THE FEDERAL TRADE COMMISSION (FTC) FRANCHISE RULE 16 CFR PARTS 436 AND 437

The Franchise Rule gives prospective purchasers of franchises the material information they need in order to weigh the risks and benefits of such an investment. The Rule requires franchisors to provide all potential franchisees with a disclosure document containing 23 specific items of information about the offered franchise, its officers, and other franchisees.

History and Overview

The FTC is the federal agency that governs how any franchise is offered for sale in the United States. It defines what a franchise is and adopts disclosure requirements and rules for offering franchises. Those FTC requirements are generally referred to as the "Franchise Rule".

The **Franchise Rule Compliance Guide** can be found here: https://www.ftc.gov/system/files/documents/plain-language/ bus70-franchise-rule-compliance-guide.pdf
[**short link:** https://bit.ly/3jdP939]

The guide spells out, in 144 pages of riveting text, exactly what you must do to become and most importantly remain a franchisor in good standing. Believe it or not, this 144-page guide doesn't cover the entirety of the rules and regulations, just the 2007 amended rule provisions.

While most states have adopted the 2008 amended Franchise Rule as presented in the cited guide, in some states the rules are still different. This might include but not be limited to filing requirements, the definition of what a franchise is, definitions of the legal relationship that govern the conduct between the franchisor and franchisee and others.

Definition of a Franchise under the Franchise Rule

Under the Franchise Rule, the FTC defines a "franchise" in Section 436.1(h) as follows: A "Franchise means any continuing commercial relationship or arrangement, whatever it may be called, in which the terms of the offer or contract specify, or the franchise seller promises or represents, orally or in writing, that: (1) The franchisee will obtain the right to operate a business that is identified or associated with the franchisor's trademark, or to offer, sell, or distribute goods, services, or commodities that are identified or associated with the franchisor's trademark; (2) The franchisor will exert or has authority to exert a significant degree of control over the franchisee's method of operation, or provide significant assistance in the franchisee's method of operation; and (3) As a condition of obtaining or commencing operation of the franchise, the franchisee makes a requirement payment or commits to make a required payment to the franchisor or its affiliate." Under a *Business Format Franchise*, the franchise relationship generally includes all the operational moving parts of the business — all its systems and processes, operating manuals, training, brand standards, quality control, a marketing strategy, etc. — and not just its logo and signage for instance.

Pre-Sale Disclosure and the Franchise Disclosure Document

The Franchise Rule requires franchisors to provide their pre-sale Franchise Disclosure Document (FDD) to prospective franchisees. According to the FTC, the Franchise Rule is *"designed to enable potential franchisees to protect themselves before investing by providing them with information essential to an assessment of the potential risks and benefits, to meaningful comparisons with other investments, and to further investigation of the franchise opportunity."* Of course, as with any such large regulation, there are significant additional and/or alternative conditions and aspects to these requirements at the federal and state level, but I am going to skip them here because they are a bit too technical for our needs right now.

Franchise Compliance

Franchisors are required to provide their completed FDD to prospective franchisees at least fourteen days prior to them signing the franchise agreement, and the franchisee is entitled to receive the completed Franchise Agreement at least seven days prior to signing it. The Rule also requires that the disclosure portion of the FDD be written in "Plain English" and not in legalese. That's good news!

23 Items

The Franchise Rule sets forth twenty-three specified areas of disclosure (called "Items" in franchise parlance):

- **Item 1:** The Franchisor and any Parents, Predecessors, and Affiliates
- **Item 2:** Business Experience
- **Item 3:** Litigation
- **Item 4:** Bankruptcy
- **Item 5:** Initial Fees
- **Item 6:** Other Fees

- **Item 7:** Estimated Initial Investment
- **Item 8:** Restrictions on Sources of Products and Services
- **Item 9:** Franchisee's Obligations
- **Item 10:** Financing
- **Item 11:** Franchisor's Assistance, Advertising, Computer Systems, and Training
- **Item 12:** Territory
- **Item 13:** Trademarks
- **Item 14:** Patents, Copyrights, and Proprietary Information
- **Item 15:** Obligation to Participate in the Actual Operation of the Franchise Business
- **Item 16:** Restrictions on What the Franchisee May Sell
- **Item 17:** Renewal, Termination, Transfer, and Dispute Resolution
- **Item 18:** Public Figures
- **Item 19:** Financial Performance Representations
- **Item 20:** Outlets and Franchisee Information
- **Item 21:** Financial Statements
- **Item 22:** Contracts
- **Item 23:** Receipts

Qualified Counsel is Essential for Both Parties

I understand (been there, done that myself) that a 'simple' business incorporation like an LLC can be handled yourself — no attorney required really. But franchisors developing the Franchise Disclosure Document should be guided by qualified franchise-experienced lawyers. For your prospective franchisees, it is important that you understand what the FDD includes and also what is not included so that you can explain those basics to your franchise candidates. While a franchisee should consult with a qualified franchise lawyer in evaluating any franchisor and to ensure clear understanding of the franchisor's offering and the franchise agreement, your job as franchisor is to prepare the FDD in plain English and with clarity.

PART TWO

How to Franchise Your Business in Four Phases

MY FOUR PHASE PROCESS TO FRANCHISING YOUR BUSINESS

Now that we've made it through the basics — from understanding terminology to seeing how the business model is federally regulated — let's dive right into the four areas that need your attention in order to franchise your business. This part of the book will present those four *phases* and the various *steps* within them.

The following chapters will break down each of the steps one by one in detail. This will all seem intimidating at first, and, no doubt about it, it can be. But the beauty of any 'process' is that it is broken down into bite-size steps that you take before proceeding to the next step, and so on.

Take your time. After a few steps, it will all make sense. Once you start following my step-by-step process for franchising your business, you will learn even more about your current business than you thought you knew.

PHASE 1: STRATEGY

This phase includes much thinking, discussing, and analyzing. This step is important and must be done before moving any further. Outlining your strategy will help you determine if you and your business are ready to franchise or not. But how do you prepare such a strategy?

We will walk you through how to do a simple step-by-step analysis on a worksheet to ensure you and your business are ready to franchise. You will want to do an initial overview of your systems, tools, software, websites, and marketing material to ensure that everything you have and are currently using is completely franchise-ready. You will review issues such as your franchising team, your competition, what makes you different, total investment, franchisee fee, royalty, training, and support that you will provide to your franchisees. This will include answering a few questions and doing some research on your top franchise competitors.

We will also estimate the time, effort, and financial input it will take for you to franchise your business. This is the final test to determine whether you are ready mentally, physically, and financially to franchise your business. We will also look at your strategy to franchise: from 100% DIY franchising, assisted via franchise development consultant, or mostly outsourced. You will have a clear path to what franchising your business will look like, what type of franchising you will offer (single vs multi), how much time it will take, and how much it will cost.

You've determined that your business is viable to franchise and have a rough idea of what your franchise will look like. This strategy phase now calls for you to write up a full-blown franchise business plan. Take all the information you have collected — your people, your infrastructure, competitive analysis, franchise fee, royalty, marketing fee, total investment, territory, training and earning potential for your franchise concept — and write it up. This document will be a 10 to 30-page overview of every aspect of your franchised model. If it doesn't make sense on paper, it won't make sense in real life. It's much better to spend the time here in this step, identifying and fixing problems, than trying to fix them with your first franchisee… or at hundreds of dollars an hour in fees with your franchise attorney.

Once you have the strategy and business plan in place, you can start the necessary process of outlining the franchisee and franchisor financial modeling. You will develop a 1 to 5-year financial projection for your franchisees based upon the existing P&L for your business. You will then look at what all of that means for you as the franchisor over the first 5 years, along with your income (sales, revenue, royalties) and your expenses as franchisor.

This strategic thinking will help you see a clear path to not only how you can help your franchisees be successful quickly but also help you to understand your financial modeling as the franchisor.

PHASE 2: LEGAL — THE FDD & FA

Franchise Disclosure Document (FDD)

In this step, we will develop responses and statements for each of the 23 required items in your Franchise Disclosure Document or FDD. This document is the backbone (or foundation if you prefer) of your entire franchise and is required by law to be given to your franchise prospects at least 14 days before they can legally become a franchisee of your concept.

The Franchise Disclosure Document for a new franchise concept typically ranges anywhere between 25 and 50 pages, and results in a well thought out presentation of your business and the opportunities it presents.

As part of this process, you will also review and do a more in-depth competitive analysis of your top franchise competitors, in order to ensure that you are in line with a great franchise program.

This initial document will be a draft to provide to the franchise attorney; even though it is not a legally binding document, it is mandated by law. Not to spook you and send you running, but the FDD document must be updated every year.

Franchise Agreement (FA)

As with the process we followed for the franchise disclosure document, you begin by writing out the elements of your Franchise Agreement (FA). This document tends to be anywhere between 50 to 100 pages for a newly formed franchisor. This is a binding contract reviewed, corrected, and completed by a qualified attorney. It is the document that you and your franchisees will sign. It outlines all aspects of the legal franchisee/franchisor relationship, and who is obligated to do what.

A franchise agreement allows both parties to agree to the terms regarding the brand, system, and expertise to be franchised. It sets the conditions of the use of the franchise system, including the term length, franchise fee and royalties, as well as other aspects such as developmental assistance, training, and marketing.

By doing this thinking and writing on your own first, you will save yourself anywhere from $5,000 to $20,000 or more in legal fees. This attorney review and updating of the FDD can take anywhere between a week, if you really nailed it, or up to 12 weeks if a lot of updating is needed.

Once the lawyers bless the documents, you're ready to develop your operational and launch strategy on when and where to register your franchise opportunity. Not all states are created equal with regard to franchising, and those specific details are presented later in this step. There are three specific types of states with regard to franchising; I will review which type your business HQ is in, and develop a strategy regarding in which states you will register your franchise.

PHASE 3: OPERATIONS – THE FRANCHISE MANUAL

Congratulations for starting from scratch and making it to this point! You have done quite a lot of thinking, strategizing, and writing. That in itself is quite an accomplishment!

The Franchise Operations Manual

This phase is about operations — the all-encompassing A-Z outline of all the moving parts of your business. You call this set of manuals the Franchise Operations and Training Manuals.

In basic terms, the Franchise Manuals are the equivalent of the Owner's Manual you get when you buy a new car. Many people (your franchisees) will take this document either printed, PDF, or online and never look at it. But there will be many who read it cover to cover and follow it to the exact word. You need to ensure it is accurate, up to date, and properly represents your business. The Operations Manual should, at its most basic, identify each franchisee's contractual obligations to you and the complete details regarding how you expect them to fulfil these obligations. When done properly, your franchisees bother you less, are more profitable, and become promoters of your franchise.

PHASE 4: LAUNCH AS FRANCHISOR — FIND FRANCHISEES

Congratulations, you are now a fully functioning franchisor! You are ready to start down the path of finding your first franchisee.

We will walk you through how to find prospects that are interested in (and qualified to) buying your franchise. You'll develop a standardized sales process: a marketing budget, decide how to put the proper people, systems, and processes in place to help automate parts of your franchise sales. You will locate the best resources on developing a franchise sales website, and finally, you will outline a budget and sales goals for your first 12 months as franchisor.

Next is your system to help your franchisee find their real estate, secure financing, handle construction, set up with all the vendors, handle the grand opening, launch their website, set up social media handles, and hire staff.

I'll help make sure you have thought through all of these items and are able to assist your franchisees like a pro through the ins and outs of smoothly getting your first franchise locations up and running.

Let's get into it, starting with Phase 1 — Strategy.

Strategy

This is an important first step and must be done before moving any further. A feasibility study — finding out whether your idea is practical or not — will help you determine if you and your business are ready to franchise or not. If franchising is not a viable growth option, you can return to the other common growth approaches discussed previously.

The Franchise Feasibility Study will walk you through how to do a simple step-by-step analysis on a worksheet to ensure that you and your business are ready to franchise.

This will include answering a few questions and doing some research on your top franchise competitors. I will help you determine your Franchise Readiness Score and, give you the green, yellow, or red-light regarding franchising your business.

You will want to do an initial review of your systems, software, websites, and marketing material to ensure that everything you have is completely franchise ready.

A WELL-KNOWN BRAND

From #10 on my own list of great franchise stories (See References and Resources section at the end of the book), I thought of **7-Eleven**.

It came to mind as I watched a YouTube video produced in and for Japan and, in the background, I saw the 7-Eleven logo on a storefront! Right there in Tokyo!

There are 60,000 franchise locations today. (Starbucks eat your heart out — it only has around 30,000). But 7-Eleven is also older, making its start fifty years earlier in 1927…mere months before the Stock Market Crash of 1929 and the Great Depression of the 1930s.

Since then, you must agree, the business has survived and thrived through prohibition, wars, recessions, and stock market ups-and-downs into the 21st century.

It all began with ice. Home and business refrigeration wasn't widespread in those days, so blocks of ice did the job. Several ice companies merged for efficiency, and the newly formed Southland Ice Company of Dallas, Texas slowly added food items and sundries to the ice they sold. Over time, they became retailers.

The name they chose indeed refers to the initial opening hours of the retail stores. They didn't expand outside of Texas until the late 1950s. Franchising began in 1964. In 1973, they licensed an affiliate in Japan, and by 1974 (one year later!) the corporation had 5,000 outlets worldwide.

I tell this story because it is important to understand that you don't need to rush and grow by hundreds or thousands of franchisees per year, even though other brands have done it. You don't have to 'go international'. You don't even have to add one franchisee per year (anytime, and especially if you are in a consolidation phase).

I also tell this story (I'm writing this during the COVID-19 shutdown days of spring 2020 and already told you how I weathered the Great Recession of 2008…) because when your concept is in high demand, the economic winds may blow, but you will be one of the likely ones that survives them.

Leave a legacy: Begin with your own solid, in-demand, profitable business. Then build, build, build — in a strategic manner.

Franchise Strategy & Budgeting

This is the final test to determine whether you are ready — mentally, physically, and financially — to franchise your business.

Once you've determined your business is ready to franchise and have a rough idea of what your franchise will look like, take a deeper dive into every aspect of your business model, your systems, processes, and software.

Review your franchising team, your competition, and what makes you different. Look at your total investment, the optimum franchisee fee, royalty, training, and support you will provide to your franchisees. Estimate the time, effort, and financial aspects of what it will take for you to franchise your business.

We will also review your options from 100% DIY franchising, assisted franchising via a franchise development consultant, or whether you mostly outsource the entire process.

You will have a clear path to what franchising your business will look like, what type of franchising you will offer (single vs multi), how much time it will take, and how much it will cost.

FOUR TYPES OF FRANCHISING OPPORTUNITIES

There are four main types of franchise arrangements or terms, which make the opportunities very flexible. Having multiple options opens franchising up to many more entrepreneurs because of the variety. Almost any observant consumer can identify them, and so can you:

- Single Unit
- Multi-Unit
- Area Developer
- Master License

The graphic below illustrates the four arrangements.

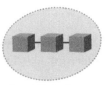

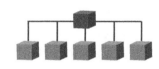

Single Unit	**Multi Unit**	**Area Developer**	**Master Franchise**
Right to open and operate ONE franchise unit	Right to open and operate more than one franchise unit	Right to open more than one unit during a specific time, within a specified area. Exclusive rights for the development of that territory.	Right to sell franchises to other people within a territory, known as sub-franchises. Receives fees and royalties. Needs to provide training and support to sub-franchises.

1) SINGLE UNIT

A single unit franchise is an agreement in which the franchisor grants the franchisee the rights to open and operate **one** franchise unit only.

This is the simplest and most common type of franchise, and many new franchisees start this way in order to 'get their feet wet'. Later, after the franchisee has launched and been successful for a time with a single unit, (s)he may negotiate with the franchisor for other units.

2) MULTI-UNIT

The franchisor grants a franchisee the rights to open and operate **more than one unit.** Typically, **there will be a pre-determined schedule** during which the franchisee will be expected to roll out or open the specified number of units. For instance, "Open the first unit within three months of the Franchise Agreement signature and starting in year two. Open two units each calendar year for a total of three years."

3) AREA DEVELOPMENT

In this agreement, the franchisor grants **exclusive territory rights to a franchisee**. As an area developer, a franchisee has the right to open more than one unit during a specific time and **within the territory**. For example, a franchisee may agree to open five units over a five-year period in the territory. The franchisor will not allow other franchisees into that territory during the term of the contract.

4) MASTER FRANCHISE

This is franchising's **'hidden gem'**. This agreement gives the franchisee **more rights** than an area development agreement. In addition to having the right and obligation to open and operate a certain number of units in a defined area, the master franchisee also **has the right to *sell* franchises to other people within the territory**. Those are known as sub-franchises. It is like being a franchisor, but in a specified territory only — sort of a 'sub-franchisor' position.

The master franchisee has the same complete support from the main franchisor, but in the territory the franchisee takes over, many of the tasks and duties of the franchisor, such as providing support and training to sub-franchisees and their employees. The master is not only acting as a franchisor in the territory, **he is able to collect his sub-franchisees' fees and royalties.**

HOW MUCH DOES FRANCHISING MY BUSINESS REALLY COST?

Here is a breakdown of the costs you will incur to franchise your business correctly and legally:

Strategy & Consulting = ($5,000 to $30,000)

The more time, energy, and effort spent here, the more money you will save on each of the items below. Many people determine in step one, during strategy and consulting meetings, that franchising is not the right fit for them.

Franchise Disclosure Document & Franchise Agreement = ($5,000 to $25,000)

I've seen this number as high as $25,000 to $50,000 if you work directly with an attorney from the start of the drafting process. The reason for the high amount is that you're paying an attorney to start you from scratch, including their billable hours for strategic planning and consulting.

This scenario is similar to when I realized that my accountant was great at taxes but was very expensive for (and frankly sucked at) bookkeeping. So, I hired a bookkeeper, and then handed my accountant the clean set of books the bookkeeper produced. This cut my time and cost by 50%.

The same logic applies here; thus, I recommend hiring a consultant to help you develop your strategy, and business model. Hand the franchise attorney of your choice a viable franchise business plan (as I handed my accountant that clean set of books) and let them add all their fancy legal mumbo jumbo and develop the documents.

These documents range anywhere between 80 to 200 pages for larger franchise brands, and typically take 30-60 days to get right. They also encompass every right, protection, or defense you have as a franchisor with a franchisee. Basically, this is the entire legally binding agreement between you and someone handing you tens of thousands of dollars.

Based on whether you are starting from scratch or already have a working plan in place, the FDD and FA typically will cost more and take longer depending on the complexity of your business, competition, and (the biggest factor) the stature and credibility of the franchise attorney or law firm you work with. As with any other area of legal practice, you pay more for bigger, reputable, and fancier law firms. I can help you navigate each option and determine which lawyer is the right fit for you.

Operations Manual = ($5,000 to $20,000)

This is the equivalent of your owner's manual when you buy a car. Basically, anything and everything an owner needs to know about the car should be in that book, including small things like tire pressure, oil type, and service intervals. Likewise, you need the owner's manual for your business — the franchisee is that owner.

The pricing here (and it includes creation of the all-important Training Manual) depends on two factors:

(1) What/if any written manuals you have already completed. Roughly 90% of my clients had no usable written Operations Manual when they came to us.

(2) The complexity of your business model. If you are picking up dog poop like the *Pet Butler* franchise, you may not need much. If you are catering and delivering theme-based Sushi rolls, you may need a live iPad version of your manual and even full how-to videos (showing everything the franchisee needs to know how to do).

State-Specific Franchise Registrations = ($0 to $10,000)

Please see my detailed breakdown in later pages — *Phase 2.3, Franchise Attorney Review and State Registrations*. Keep in mind that states modify their business registration criteria periodically, so it is the state office which you must question directly when you are preparing to register.

Franchise Sales, Marketing & PR for at least six months = ($6,000 to $60,000)

That is your budget per month for at least six months, depending on your franchise sales goal.

See *Phase 4.1 — Franchise Sales & Marketing* in later pages for more details.

Total:

Process	Low Investment	High Investment	Paid To
Strategy Consulting	$5,000	$30,000	Consultant
FDD & FA	$5,000	$25,000	Lawyer
Operations/Training Manuals	$5,000	$20,000	Consultant
State Registrations	$0	$10,000	Lawyer
6 Months (Leads & PR)	$6,000	$60,000	Marketing Co's
Total	$21,000	$145,000	

HOW LONG WILL IT TAKE TO FRANCHISE MY BUSINESS?

Let's say preparation and paperwork time = 3-6 months on average.

I have had clients in non-registration states (see that section) that have completed the process in as little as 45 days. Usually in this scenario, the company already has a prospect — employee or family member — lined up to be the first franchisee.

The other scenario is when I am working with a company that is getting ready to sell, and they are completing the basic requirements to sell their entire business, or several existing locations as franchises vs outright or straight business sales.

In a normal scenario, however, if you are starting from scratch, your typical process takes between 3-6 months — depending on how much energy and effort you can put into the project, and how well documented your systems and processes are when you begin.

The Franchise Business Plan

Now it's time to put all your fabulous ideas and clear concepts on to paper and write up a full-blown franchise business plan. Yes, many startup businesses do so 'by the seat of their pants', but franchisors decidedly must plan and strategize — and write up the resulting franchise business plan.

This plan will cover every aspect of your business: your people, your infrastructure, competitive analysis, franchise fees, royalty, marketing fees, total investment, territory, training and earning potential for your franchise concept.

This document will assist you in the later phases of this process, so I urge you to take this step quite seriously — get help by assigning tasks to employees to participate in building the plan.

This document will be a 10 to 30-page overview of every aspect of your franchised model — and if it doesn't make sense on paper, it won't make sense in real life. It's much better to spend the time here in this step fixing problems than trying to fix them later, either with your first franchisee or at the cost of hundreds of dollars an hour with your franchise attorney.

"Failing to Plan is Planning to Fail", as the adage goes. In this scenario, I've seen people invest $100,000+ in franchising their business before they really had a solid plan in writing. If they had drafted the plan (accompanied by all the thinking and information-collection it entails) on the true viability of their business as a franchise, they would perhaps have spent less money! They didn't understand the competitive landscape; they didn't understand the method to go to market; they didn't understand the financial modeling of a franchisor.

You, my friend, will not be this person. DO NOT FRANCHISE YOUR BUSINESS until you have completed a franchise strategy and its business plan. Not doing so would be like trying to build a house and skipping working with an architect.

The business plan should at minimum cover the following aspects of your business in a ½-1 page narrative explanation per item:

- Overview of Your Business Model
- Products & Services You Offer
- Your Team/Organization Org Chart with Roles & Responsibilities
- Legal Structure of Your Franchise
- Trademarks (or when you plan on obtaining them)
- Competitor Review of at least (3) competitors, including the following:
  - Name
  - Year Started Franchising
  - Number of Locations franchised (vs corporate-reserved locations)
  - Franchise Fee
  - Royalties
  - Number of Lawsuits
  - Training
  - Financial Overview
- Your Franchising Goals: Sales & Operationally
- Your Franchising Strategy
  - Single Unit
  - Area Developer
  - Master License
- Ideal Candidate for Your Franchise & Targeting Strategy
- Territory Overview
- Your Training Program
  - How Long

- Where Is It Conducted?
- Who Does What?
- Your Support Capacity
  - Who Is in Charge of Support?
- Ticketing Systems
- Operational Support
- Marketing Support
- Sales Assistance
- Site Selection/Real Estate (if required)
- Financing
- Purchasing
- Legal
- Bookkeeping/Audit
- Ongoing R&D
- Default, Termination & Resale
- Financial Modeling
- Franchise Fee
- Royalties
- Item 5 of the FDD
- Item 6 of FDD
- Item 7 of FDD
- Franchisee Total Investment
- Franchisee Working Capital
- Franchise Duration/Term
- Additional Investments Needed?
- Vendors & Supplier Review
- Item 19 Review for FDD (How much money can a franchisee make)
- Franchisor Financial Modeling
- Franchisee Financial Modeling
- Conclusion/Review

HOW TO DETERMINE YOUR FRANCHISE FEE

The methodology for fee determination calls for franchisors to look to their franchise fees primarily as *cost recovery* tools and only secondarily as *profit centers*. Franchisors would obviously like to maximize their franchise fee revenue, but knowing the importance of establishing the associated royalties, most franchisors price their fees low enough to avoid erecting barriers to the franchise sale. In determining franchise fees, three approaches in particular can be used simultaneously. They are the Cost-Plus, the Competitive Value Approach, and the Perceived Value Approach.

Before we start this exercise, it is important to note that there is no legal requirement for you to charge a franchise fee. If you decide that you want to give away your franchise for free, you have the right to do so.

I have worked with clients who have considered this approach. They were going to raise the royalties to a higher percentage in lieu of an upfront fee. This client was in the tax preparation business, and we recommended against giving it away. The main reason is that most people do not see value in something that they get for free.

We decided to go with the Competitive Approach, and their main competitor was the tax preparation franchise H&R Block with 10,000+ locations. Their franchise fee in 2020 is a whopping $2,500, but their royalty starts at 60%. Yes, you read that right! The franchise fee is $2,500, and their royalties start at 60%. Our client decided to go with a $1,250 franchise fee and 30% royalties. This allowed them to state that they charged 50% less than their main competitor.

With that point made, let's walk through the differences between the three approaches to creating your franchise fee. We recommend trying and comparing all three approaches before finalizing your franchise fee.

Cost-Plus Approach

The table on the next page is a real example of a Cost-Plus Approach to the franchisee fee that we created for a moving company. With this approach, the goal is to estimate all your initial expenses of selling and setting up your franchisee. Using that information, you can determine a low and high franchisee fee amount. For this client, we used $15,000 as the low franchise fee and $60,000 for the high. As mentioned in the previous section, this amount can vary drastically based upon your industry.

Description of Service	Time	Cost (Low)	Cost (High)
Initial Training at Your Location	1-3 weeks	$2,000	$5,000
Onsite Training (Franchisee's Location)	1-2 weeks	$2,000	$5,000
Lead Generation Marketing Cost	1 time	$0	$20,000
Internal Sales Commission	1 time	$0	$10,000
Broker Referral Fee	1 time	$0	$25,000
Total Expense		$4,000	$65,000
Franchise Fee		$15,000	$60,000
Free Cash Flow from Franchise Fee		$11,000	-$5,000

You can see that on the low end, the expense for setting up and training a new franchisee was $4,000. In this scenario, you would be selling a franchise to someone you already know. So, there is no expense allocated for marketing, commissions, or referral fees. On the high end, the total expense was $65,000.

On the low end, with only a $15,000 franchise fee, a profit of $11,000 could still be made. On the high end, with a franchise fee of $60,000, the expenses could be $65,000. This would mean a $5,000 loss on the sale of a franchise.

In the high end scenario, it would cost them $5,000 to open a new location as a franchise. In contrast, it would cost them $300,000 to open a new location on their own, not counting the additional costs for employees and liabilities.

With a $5,000 loss on the franchise sale divided by a 6% royalty, they would need the franchisee to make $83,333 in revenue (ever) to break even on the sale of that franchise. That's $83,333 (franchisee revenue) x 6% (royalty) = $5,000 in revenue to you as the franchisor.

The goal with this approach is to test the low and high limits of your franchise fee and settle on a happy medium that you can live with on paper. You can always change this number upon renewing or amending your FDD. However, you want to avoid, for obvious reasons, starting at $50,000 and then dropping it to $15,000 the next year.

Competitive Approach

The competitive approach requires us to do some legwork and research the franchise fees of your top three to four franchise competitors. You can find free FDDs by going to the resource center at **www.HowToFranchiseBook.com** or by searching online for "Free FDD Search."

For the moving company, we selected the following three companies to compare their franchise fees.

- Two Men and a Truck = $50,000 to $85,000
- Northstar Moving = $50,000
- College Hunks Hauling Junk = $40,000 to $50,000

The first thing you will notice is that two of the three companies have a range for the franchise fee. With the Two Men franchise, you pay $50,000 for a market they are not already established in and $85,000 for a market that they are.

College Hunks has two separate concepts that they franchise with one FDD: The junk hauling business and the moving business. You pay $40,000 for just the junk hauling, or you pay a $50,000 initial franchise fee for both the junk hauling and moving brand. So, for $10,000 more, you get two business models versus one.

Side Note: For your first year or two of franchising, I do not recommend having this level of complexity in your initial franchise fees. We highly recommend making it one standard flat amount.

With that exercise done, we can use some very simple math to determine the average franchise fee for moving companies.

$$\$50,000 + \$50,000 + \$40,000 = \$140,000 \mathbin{/} 3 = \$46,666$$

Using this approach, we decided on a $35,000 franchise fee to be competitive against the big brands, coming in just slightly below the smaller but well-established player. We also recommend going back to the table in the Cost-Plus Approach section and plugging in $35,000 to the franchisee fee column.

On the low end, with only $4,000 in expenses, a $35,000 franchise fee would produce a $31,000 profit. On the high end, with $65,000 in expenses, this would produce a $30,000 loss. That amount of loss would be unacceptable, so we would have to reduce or eliminate internal sales commissions and/or broker referral fees.

Perceived Value Approach

Although relatively few examples exist of companies entering franchising with a high degree of name recognition, those that do can position their offering toward the high end of the competitive spectrum. The best example for a brand that would have perceived value would be In-N-Out Burger. Since they opened in 1948, they have held out from franchising, even though hundreds of thousands of people have requested that they do.

The heir to the burger giant, Lynsi Snyder, has become a billionaire off the fast casual food chain. Since they are privately owned, nobody knows exactly, but it's estimated that they do $575 million in annual revenue from their 350+ locations. These are very impressive numbers for a nearly 80-year iconic West Coast brand. If they were to franchise, the Perceived Value Approach would be the way to go. If your business has a perceived value in your local market or region, that allows you to use this approach.

Premium positioning is not a license to charge more than the market price in the face of established successful franchise competition. It is, however, grounds to avoid the 'low, low introductory' pricing that beginning franchisors often charge to get a foothold in the market in a field dominated by a few big names.

Taking each of these elements into account, in addition to the financial results that the franchisor expects franchisees to achieve, its positioning in the industry, sales goals, and the level of support it intends to provide, a franchise fee of $50,000 will be charged by this moving company franchisor, and this is for both startup franchises and conversion models. This fee is to be paid at the signing of the Franchise Agreement, where applicable.

HOW TO DETERMINE YOUR ROYALTY FEE

For the process of selecting your royalty fee, we simply use the Competitive Approach. Using the moving company again as an example, we can review the same three competitors to determine what they charge in royalties.

- Two Men and a Truck = 6%

- Northstar Moving = 8%

- College Hunks Hauling Junk = 7%

So that's 7% (6 + 8 + 7 = 21 / 3 = 7%) average in royalties between the three brands. With the number right in the middle, how do we pick what is best between the three? When there is a deadlock like this during any of our reviews, the next section of the FDD I look to compare is *Item 20 – Outlets and Franchisee Information*.

This section will tell us who has the most franchisees in their system, and those numbers are listed below.

- Two Men and a Truck = 276 locations

- Northstar Moving = 3 locations

- College Hunks Hauling Junk = 117 locations

Northstar, with three locations, charges 2% more in royalties than Two Men and a Truck, which is the largest player in the space and has the same franchise fee. College Hunks charges 1% less than Northstar, and for the same franchise fee of $50,000, College Hunks gives you two business opportunities — moving and junk hauling.

Hopefully, you can see why the Northstar franchise has struggled to sell and compete against these larger well-established players in this space. Working through this process will ensure that this doesn't happen to your franchise brand.

For our client, we landed on and recommended a 6% royalty fee to be in line with Two Men and a Truck. We are able to say that in established markets for Two Men, which is every major city in America, our franchise fee is $50,000 less, and we charge the same royalty amount.

BONUS FRANCHISE STORY: McDonald's vs. In-N-Out

To help contrast franchising versus not franchising, here is a story of two iconic American brands. Let's quickly compare the history of In-N-Out to McDonald's. As mentioned earlier, the first In-N-Out opened in Baldwin Park, CA, back in 1948. That same year, just 14 miles away in Downey, CA, Richard and Maurice (the McDonald brothers) shut down their BBQ joint for three months and opened back up as McDonald's. Five years later in 1953, McDonald's started franchising, and in 1954, In-N-Out updated their logo.

In 1970, In-N-Out introduced character glasses at their restaurants. That same year, McDonald's opened their 1,000th location. In 1990, In-N-Out opened their 64th location, and McDonald's opened their 10,000th location. In 2008 — the 60th anniversary of both companies — In-N-Out had grown to 224 locations in California, Nevada, Arizona, and Utah. That same year, McDonald's was in 100 countries with 35,000 locations.

Today, McDonald's has roughly 40,000 locations, does $21 billion in annual revenue, and is publicly traded on the New York Stock Exchange. In-N-Out has 350+ locations and an estimated $575 million in annual revenue, or roughly 0.9% of the locations and 3% of the total annual revenue compared to McDonald's.

I am making no judgement here. Both companies have created billionaires from the business and are iconic American brands. But these two companies started in the same year, 14 miles apart from each other, in the same exact industry. Which would you rather be? That choice is up to you to decide...

Franchisee & Franchisor Financial Modeling

Once you have the strategy and written business plan in place, you can start the necessary process of outlining the franchisee and franchisor financial modeling.

What this entails is developing a 1-5 year financial projection for your franchisees based upon the existing (historic) P&L for your business.

Like with the business plan, you look at all of the numbers from a 'startup business' perspective, because your franchisor operations are indeed a startup. Look at the franchisor operations from startup and over the first 5 years. Analyze and estimate income from franchise sales, royalties, and any additional revenue (example: additional procurement, project management, and other fees) and most importantly outline the most common expenses you will have.

This will help you see a clear path to not only how your franchisees be successful but also help you to understand your financial modeling as the franchisor.

HOW MUCH MONEY CAN A FRANCHISOR & FRANCHISEES MAKE?

Here is the Bottom Line: The business opportunity you present must make sense for both you as the franchisor, and also, more importantly, for your franchisees.

Nothing spells disaster faster (even though that has a great buzz) than developing a financial model that is a Win/Lose opportunity for either the franchisee or the franchisor. In the short-term — say your first 10 franchisees or roughly the first year of your franchise offering — the model should be more one-sided to the franchisee to help ensure they are successful. There will be a lot of work or effort on your end as well, so it must make short-term financial sense for you too.

I have also seen franchisors who are not so transparent with how they are making their money. This could be in the form of kickbacks or vendor rebates that may or may not have been properly disclosed. Transparency and fairness are key here to ensuring outstanding commercial relationships with your franchisees and the financial success of the franchisor organization.

FRANCHISEE PROFITABILITY

To best understand the profit potential for a franchisee, it's important to understand how to read an "Item 19: Financial Performance Representation". To do that, I have outlined the "Item 19s" from two well-known franchise concepts. It's important to note there is no set way to state these numbers in your FDD, and it is not required that you make an "earnings claim" in your FDD. But it's even more important to understand that you can only state financial projections or numbers based on what you have in your FDD.

So, in laymen's terms, if you're selling your first franchise, and the potential franchisee asks, "how much money can I make?", you can only show/tell them exactly what's in your Item 19. You cannot email them over your P&L for last month or forward them the last big deal closed. If you decide not to have an earnings claim and you do not have a franchisee they can speak with, your answer has to be "sorry we don't make any financial performance representations at this time."

With that, let's contrast and compare summaries of the Item 19's of two well-known franchise concepts: Anytime Fitness and Pizza Hut.

Anytime Fitness (2019 FDD) Quick Facts:

- Franchise Fee = $42,500 from Item 5: Initial Fees
- Royalty = Flat Fee of $699 per month from Item 6: Other Fees

- Total Investment = $78,000 to $522,000 from Item 7: Estimated Initial Investment

- # of US Franchisees = 2451 from Item 20: Outlets and Franchise Information

So for your $78,000 up to $522,000 total initial investment, how can you determine what your potential ROI on your Anytime Fitness would be? For that, we are going to look at what's listed in their 2019 Item 19: Financial Performance Representation.

Anytime Fitness (2019 FDD) Item 19 Summary:

Below is verbatim from their FDD:

The following are statements of projected annual revenues and earnings for a franchised Anytime Fitness center. These projections are for an Anytime Fitness center that has been in operation for at least 12 months. They assume that at the end of the first year you have a fixed number of memberships, and, even though most of our clubs continue to increase their memberships after the first year, that you remain at that level for the entire year, adding as many new members as the number of members that leave. (During the first year, it will take you time to build your member base). We have listed below three projections: one based on a center having 500 members, one based on 860 members, and one based on 1,150 members. They are based on revenue information provided to us by our proprietary software and designated billing processor for our franchisees in the United States in 2018.

Of the 2,235 Anytime Fitness clubs open for at least 12 months as of February 28, 2019, the number of members for these clubs ranged from 145 to 3,418. As measured on February 28, 2019, the clubs open at least 12 months had an average member count of 860; the member count on this date ranged from 136 to 3,402 and the median was 776.

The first example, for a 500-member club, is intended to give you an idea of the revenues, expenses, and projected income of a club that performs well below our average but is still profitable. Of these

2,235 clubs, 1,909 (85%) had an average of over 500 members as measured on February 28, 2019. The 860-member example will give you an idea of the revenues, expenses, and income of a club that is able to maintain, throughout the year, the average number of members of the Anytime Fitness clubs that were open for at least 12 months, as measured on February 28, 2019. Of the 2,235 Anytime Fitness clubs open for at least 12 months as of February 28, 2019, 887 (40%) had an average of over 860 members, as measured on February 28, 2019. The 1,150-member example gives you an idea of the revenues, expenses, and profitability of a high achieving club. Of the 2,235 Anytime Fitness clubs open for at least 12 months as of February 28, 2019, 391 (17%) had an average of over 1,150 members as measured on February 28, 2019.

The assumptions we made in compiling these projections are detailed following the projections. Any change in these assumptions would require material alterations to the projections.

	500 Members	860 Members	1,150 Members
Revenues[1]			
Enrollment Fee[2]	$13,500	$23,200	$31,000
Membership Fees[3,4]	$183,100	$315,000	$421,200
Vending Revenues[5]	$1,500	$2,600	$3,500
Personal Training[6]	$52,100	$89,500	$119,700
Total Revenues[7]	$250,200	$430,300	$575,400
Operating Expenses[1]			
Rent[8]	$95,600	$95,600	$95,600
Personal Training Expenses[6]	$31,300	$53,700	$83,800
Royalties	$8,400	$8,400	$8,400
Processing/Credit Card Fees[9]	$10,100	$17,400	$23,300
Bad Debt[10]	$6,100	$10,400	$13,900
Utilities[11]	$21,700	$21,700	$21,700
Insurance	$2,500	$2,500	$2,500
Proximity Cards[2,3]	$1,600	$2,700	$3,600
Advertising Funds[12]	$7,200	$7,200	$7,200
Local Advertising[13]	$10,000	$12,700	$14,900
Vending Products[5]	$500	$800	$1,100
Maintenance	$7,900	$13,700	$18,300
Base Technology Fee[14]	$9,600	$9,600	$9,600
Healthy Contribution Fees[15]	$300	$500	$700

Conference Fee	$200	$200	$200
Miscellaneous[16,18]	$8,100	$13,500	$17,900
Total Operating Expenses	$221,100	$270,600	$322,700
Income Before Salaries, Depreciation, Interest, Taxes and Debt Expense[17]	$29,100	$159,700	$252,700
Manager(s) Salary and Payroll Costs17		$45,900	$45,900
Income Before Depreciation, Interest, Taxes and Debt Expense[17, 18]	$29,100	$113,800	$206,800

As you can see, Anytime Fitness shows an annualized example breakdown of three identical rent (largest expense) locations, with differing numbers of members. One with 500 members and $250,200 in revenue, another with 860 members and $430,300 in revenue, and the third with 1150 members and $575,400 in revenue. What many franchisees look for is the capacity to make more than what they were making at their job or previous roles. This can quickly show you what level you will need to grow the business to in order to accomplish that. If you're looking to make $100K plus, you will need on average 860 members to hit that number. I also like to simplify the P&L by breaking down the revenue, expenses, and profit per member as follows.

Average Annual Revenue Per Member:

- $250,200/500 = $500

- $430,300/860 = $500

- $575,400/1150 = $500

Average Annual Expense Per Member:

- $221,100/500 = $442

- $270,600/860 = $315

- $322,700/1150 = $280

Average Annual Profit Per Member:

- $29,100/500 = $58

- $113,800/860 = $132

- $206,800/1150 = $180

What this allows you to quickly see is that while revenue per member is static, your expenses per member drops significantly and your profit per member nearly triples at scale. With that exercise done, we can run several quick financial models. It is also very important to note that with 500 members, they don't have a line item for managers or employees (beyond personal trainers), which means you are expected to be the one running it. With the Anytime Fitness Item 19, you can work with your accountant to build out a financial proforma based upon historical averages.

What does the Anytime Fitness income statement for this year look like?

ANYTIME FITNESS, LLC
STATEMENTS OF INCOME   **Statement 2**
December 31, 2018, 2017 and 2016

	2018	2017	2016
Revenues:			
Monthly franchise fees	$21,140,680	$18,873,844	$16,616,589
Initial franchise fees	9,812,687	9,543,958	9,788,827
Area development fee	1,711,500	2,364,500	2,275,500
Master franchise fee	500,000	200,000	40,000
Sales	13,819,460	14,639,506	14,202,906
Vendor rebates	34,230,627	22,176,794	16,939,767
Other revenues	1,492,427	640,945	477,985
Total revenues	82,707,381	68,439,547	60,341,574
Cost of goods sold	3,187,100	3,344,226	3,012,160
Gross profit	79,520,281	65,095,321	57,329,414
General and administrative expenses	40,246,238	37,609,655	34,407,716
Income from operations	39,274,043	27,485,666	22,921,698
Other income (expense):			
Interest expense	(17,693)	(21,122)	(40,962)
Other income	16,664	27,239	43,277
Other expense	(1,284,342)	(889,089)	(691,010)
Gain (loss) on sale of club operations	123,096	(129,468)	-
Total other expense	(1,162,275)	(1,012,440)	(688,695)
Net income	$38,111,768	$26,473,226	$22,233,003

As you can see, Anytime Fitness brought in $21M in monthly franchisee/royalty fees, $9.8M in initial franchise fees, and $34M in Vendor Rebates. Let's focus on that for a minute. They made roughly $31M in royalty and franchise fees, but they made $34M in vendor rebates. In total, they brought in $82M with a net income of $38M or 46% to the bottom line.

Pizza Hut (2020 FDD) Quick Facts:

- Franchise Fee = $25,000 from Item 5: Initial Fees
- Royalty = 6% from Item 6: Other Fees
- Total Investment = $787,000 to $2,100,000 from Item 7: Estimated Initial Investment
- # of US Franchisees = 5976 from Item 20: Outlets and Franchise Information

So for $787k to $2.1M, how much money does Pizza Hut say you can make in return? Let's take a look at a summary of their Item 19: Financial Performance Representation.

Pizza Hut (2020 FDD) Item 19 Summary. Below is verbatim from their FDD:

ITEM 19
FINANCIAL PERFORMANCE REPRESENTATIONS

The FTC's Franchise Rule permits a franchisor to provide information about the actual or potential financial performance of its franchised and/or franchisor-owned outlets, if there is a reasonable basis for the information, and if the information is included in the disclosure document. Financial performance information that differs from that included in Item 19 may be given only if: (1) a franchisor provides the actual records of an existing outlet you are considering buying; or (2) a franchisor supplements the information provided in this Item 19, for example, by providing information about possible performance at a particular location or under particular circumstances.

Set forth below are historical data for certain domestic traditional Pizza Hut outlets owned and operated by us or our affiliates ("Company-Owned System Restaurants") and certain domestic traditional Pizza Hut outlets owned and operated by franchisees ("Franchised System Restaurants").

I.　　MATURE COMPANY-OWNED SYSTEM RESTAURANTS

The financial performance representations below provide certain information regarding Company-Owned RBD and Delco System Restaurants that were open and operating for at least one year as of December 31, 2019 and that were situated on leased real property ("Mature Company Owned System Restaurants"). Specifically excluded from Mature Company-Owned System Restaurants are System Restaurants for which PHLLC or its affiliates owned the real property; Carryout-only System Restaurants; seasonal System Restaurants; Express restaurants (for which licenses are offered under a separate disclosure document); or, any type of System Restaurant other than traditional RBD and Delco System Restaurants. As of December 31, 2019, there were 21 Mature Company-Owned System Restaurants, which are reflected in the subset information provided below. No Company-Owned System Restaurants closed in 2019.

2019 Average Performance – Mature Company Owned System Restaurants

Ownership/Concept	Count	Average Gross Sales (Note 1)	Median Gross Sales	Average Cost of Sales (Note 2)	Product as % of Gross Sales	Average cost of Labor (Note 3)	Labor as % of Gross Sales
Mature Company-Owned System Restaurants	21	$883,383	$917,346	$242,080	27.4%	$281,546	31.9%

II.   MATURE FRANCHISED SYSTEM RESTAURANTS

The financial performance representations below provide certain information regarding the Franchised System Restaurants – of the Dine-In/Red Roof, RBD and Delco Delivery/Carry-out Restaurant Concept type – that were open and operating for at least one year as of December 31, 2019 ("Mature Franchised System Restaurants"). Specifically excluded from the definition of Mature Franchised System Restaurants are those DBR/FCD System Restaurants; Carryout-only System Restaurants; seasonal System Restaurants; Express restaurants (for which franchises are offered under a separate disclosure document); any type of System Restaurant that reported sales for 24 or fewer days in each financial period; or, any type of System Restaurant other than traditional Dine-In/Red Roof, RBD and Delco Delivery/Carry-out System Restaurants. As of December 31, 2019, although there were a total of 5,922 Franchised System Restaurants, there were 5,665 Mature Franchised System Restaurants. The table below excludes 165 Mature Franchised System Restaurants that closed in 2019.

Mature Franchised System Restaurants of the Dine-In/Red Roof and RBD Restaurant Concept Type

Ownership/Concept	Count	Average Gross Sales (Note 1)	Median Gross Sales
Mature Franchised System Restaurants of the Dine-In/Red Roof and RBD Restaurant Concept Type	2,751	$939,500	$879,492

Mature Franchised System Restaurants of the Delco Delivery/Carry-out Restaurant Concept Type

Ownership/Concept	Count	Average Gross Sales (Note 1)	Median Gross Sales
Mature Franchised System Restaurants of the Delco Delivery/Carry-out Restaurant Concept Type	2,914	$863,538	$822,661

2019 Average Performance – All Mature Franchise System Restaurants

Ownership/Concept	Count	Average Gross Sales (Note 1)	Median Gross Sales
All Mature Franchised Restaurants	5,665	$900,426	$849,830

As you can see, Pizza Hut's Item 19 in no way resembles Anytime Fitness. Not just because one is a gym and one is a pizza business, but because there is no standard protocol for what, or how, you state your financial performance representation, if you make one at all. Pizza Hut gives you average cost of sales and labor for their 21 corporate locations but doesn't give that on their 5665 "Mature Franchised Restaurants". What's a Mature Franchised Restaurant? They list it above as a location that was open for at least one year on 12/31/2019. So any location that opened in 2020 is not included on this chart.

That means you should not expect to reach these averages within your first 12 months of business at a minimum. But a quick Google search will let you know that Pizza Hut has been franchising since 1960, or 80 years now at this point, which means within the 5,665 franchises are locations that may be 80 years in business — literally.

What does Pizza Hut get for creating all those commercials and supporting 5,500+ franchise locations in the United States? Let's take a look at their audited income statements (from their 2020 FDD) to find out. Each franchisor also has a balance sheet that gets posted into the FDD as well. But 99% of the time, as a new franchisor, we recommend you start a new entity and new bank account for clean accounting and a simple balance sheet and income statement. There are some states with certain balance sheet requirements, and we recommend discussing this topic with your lawyer and accountant.

Pizza Hut Guarantor, LLC and Subsidiary
Consolidated Statements of Income
Fiscal years ended December 30, 2019, December 24, 2018 and December 25, 2017
(In thousands)

	2019	2018	2017
Revenues:			
Franchise and license revenues	$ 282,777	$ 285,087	$ 263,469
Franchise contributions for advertising and other services	273,425	250,284	-
Total revenues	556,202	535,371	263,469
Costs and expenses:			
General and administrative expenses (Note 5)	76,374	71,045	69,283
Franchise and license expenses (Note 5)	24,983	27,473	53,888
Franchise advertising and other services expense	278,949	260,074	-
Total costs and expenses	380,306	358,592	123,171
Other income	701	753	-
Net Income	$ 176,597	$ 177,532	$ 140,298

See accompanying notes to consolidated financial statements

As you can see, Pizza Hut brought in $556M in revenue from franchisees in 2019 and had $380M in expenses. So in 2019, they brought in $177M or 32% of revenue to the bottom line.

I picked these two concepts to show you that there is not one set way to display your financial modeling to a perspective franchisee. But as a new startup franchisor, I recommend simply putting in a clean, audited year end P&L, simulating the royalty payment, and keeping all else equal.

Legal

Creating a business in the USA is always going to require you to address some legalities. When you founded your own business, you surely incorporated it as a protective measure. To grow this same business as a franchisor, there are additional layers of legal steps to take — and they each likewise serve to protect the parties involved. The franchisee and you get protection from, in particular, two types of legal, signed documents.

Never skip available legal protections! Separation of business entities from your personal assets is crucial for many good reasons. From Denny's to Choice Hotels to Pella Windows, franchisors do get in legal trouble. Trouble is not a given when you get legal counsel before launch; understand all the legal obligations you are entering into and ethically respect the agreements you have signed.

But you also need legal protections and advice when no trouble is on the horizon. You may just be managing, divesting, merging, and acquiring several businesses in the most efficient manner, as this following story partially demonstrates.

A WELL-KNOWN BRAND

My favorite story about a franchise that made its way through many legal formations and reformations and still remains strong today is the Hilton Hotel story.

This is not a start-from-scratch story. Conrad N. Hilton bought a small Texas inn in 1919. From that purchase, he grew the Hilton Hotels Corporation. Conrad Hilton's sons later followed their father into business. They gradually grew the number of their hotel locations. Then new business additions began.

In 1959, Conrad Hilton started the Carte Blanche credit card business, with son Barron in charge. The company lost $2 million in six years, before it was sold to Citibank. Barron was very interested in making gambling a part of the Hilton empire, and moved the company's focus away from hotels. In 1964, the company spun off its international hotels to shareholders because Barron argued that the parts were worth more than the whole, a move that some questioned. In 1967, Barron convinced his father, the biggest stockholder of Hilton International, to sell his shares to Trans World Airlines (TWA) in exchange for that company's stock.

All those permutations of the 'family business' required legal consultations, documentations, registrations, and protections available through the law.

While there is no reason not to expand the scope of a business, it is not typically what is done in the franchising world. Read on for the initial (and simpler than what Barron Hilton took his business through) legal formalities of becoming a franchisor.

Franchise Disclosure Document (FDD)

I n this step, you will provide the information for the 23 required items found in your *Franchise Disclosure Document*.

This document — the FDD — is the backbone of your entire franchise and is required by law to be given to your franchise prospects as part of the pre-sale due diligence process at least 14 days before they can legally become a franchisee of your concept. The FDD typically ranges anywhere between 25 and 50 pages. This initial FDD document that you end up with will be the draft you provide to your chosen franchise attorney.

UNDERSTANDING THE FRANCHISE DISCLOSURE DOCUMENT

The FDD provides comprehensive information about the franchisor and thus allows the franchisee to make an informed decision on whether or not to work with the organization. The FDD is an agreement about a franchise opportunity and information about the franchisor. The FDD is not a legally binding contract — hence the name 'document'. Its terms may change annually as the franchisor organization grows and evolves (see next section Franchisor Agreement for the binding contract).

Sections of the FDD

The FDD discloses information about the franchisor that is essential to potential franchisees about how to make a significant investment:

- **Item 1:** The franchisor and any parents, predecessors, and affiliates

- **Item 2:** Business experience

- **Item 3:** Litigation

- **Item 4:** Bankruptcy

- **Item 5:** Initial fees: A franchisor must disclose any fees charged to franchisees.

- **Item 6:** Other fees: This section must also include any other fees. Any hidden or undisclosed fees can be a source of dispute later on down the road, so a franchisor must be careful and fully transparent.

- **Item 7:** Estimated initial investment: The franchisee must be aware of what the low and high range of the initial investment must be, including an estimate of his working capital.

- **Item 8:** Restrictions on sources of products and services

- **Item 9:** Franchisee's obligations

- **Item 10:** Financing

- **Item 11:** Franchisor's assistance, advertising, computer systems, and training

- **Item 12:** Territory: While there is no obligation to give a franchisee any range or territory to do business, this is the space to indicate any geographical restrictions a franchisor is putting on the franchisee.

- **Item 13:** Trademarks

- **Item 14:** Patents, copyrights, and proprietary information

- **Item 15:** Obligation to participate in the actual operation of the franchise business

- **Item 16:** Restrictions on what the franchisee may sell

- **Item 17:** Renewal, termination, transfer, and dispute resolution

- **Item 18:** Public figures

- **Item 19:** Financial performance representations

- **Item 20:** Outlets and franchisee information

- **Item 21:** Financial statements: A franchisor must provide three years of financial statements to the franchisee as part of the financial disclosure document. This includes balance sheets, statements of operations, owner's equity, and cash flows.

- **Item 22:** Contracts: This is where the franchisor outlines the franchise agreement. It may also include financing agreements, product supply agreements, personal guarantees, software licensing agreements, and any other contracts specific to the franchise's situation.

- **Item 23:** Receipts: This is the last and final section of the FDD. Here, the franchisor will review the disclosure and business decisions outlined between the two parties and provide the franchisee with any additional information.

Franchise Agreement (FA)

As with the process you followed for the Franchise Disclosure Document, you will detail your working contract points in a separate **Franchise Agreement (FA)**.

This legally binding document tends to be anywhere between 50 and 100 pages for a newly formed franchisor. Unlike the FDD, this contract and its terms rarely change over the life of the franchise arrangement between the signatories. This is the document your franchisees will sign, and outlines all aspects of the franchisee/franchisor relationship, along with each party's privileges, obligations, and rights.

WHAT IS A FRANCHISE AGREEMENT?

A Franchise Agreement or FA, once signed by both parties, is a legally binding contract. It allows both parties to agree to the terms regarding the brand, operational system, and expertise to be franchised. The FA sets the conditions of the use of the franchise system as franchisee, including the term length, initial franchise fee, royalties and periodicity, developmental assistance, training, and marketing. It also goes into detail on how the franchisee obtains and retains the right to utilize the franchisor's trademarks, trade dress, business systems, Operations Manual, and sources of supply in offering and selling the products and/or services designated by the franchisor.

The Franchise Agreement must be legally disclosed as an exhibit (addendum, for review) to a franchisor's Franchise Disclosure Document.

RIGHTS DEFINED BY FRANCHISE AGREEMENTS

As a franchisor, your franchise agreement will serve as the primary and most important legal document to govern and define the legal relationship with your franchisees. Within your franchise agreement, you will be granting your franchisees the legal right to establish and develop their franchised locations and, in turn, the franchisees will be undertaking the obligation to establish and maintain their franchised operations in accordance with the mandates of your system, and to pay to you certain ongoing fees.

On the franchisee or prospective franchisee side, the FA is the most critical document in your franchise investment packet. If you are verbally promising something, the franchisee must make sure you are able to execute on this promise and will expect to see it in writing in the FA.

Everything you agree to do must be contained in the franchise agreement or an amendment to the franchise agreement.

Within your franchise agreement, some of the substantive legal rights and obligations that will be established include the following:

The Grant of Franchise Rights and Term. This is the right to establish and operate a franchised location or outlet, including the license to utilize the franchisor's trademarks, trade dress, and business systems. Typically, franchise rights are granted for a term of 10 years but do vary.

Franchisee's Development Obligations. The franchisee's obligation to establish and commence (open for business) a franchised location or locations and the date by which to do so.

Initial and Continuing Training. The initial training the franchisor will provide to the franchisee prior to opening and any ongoing training offered or required by the Franchisor.

Territorial Rights. Whether or not the franchisee is granted a form of territorial protection wherein, for example, the franchisor will not grant competing franchises. Typically, franchisees will be granted an operating territory. The franchise agreement will define where the franchisee may operate the franchised business, who the franchisee may or may not sell products or service to and any protection that may be afforded to the franchisee regarding their territory.

Operating Procedures. The franchise agreement will require that the franchisee follow the systems and procedures established by the franchisor, only offer and sell those products and services authorized by the franchisor, and follow the mandates and operating procedures contained in the franchisor's Operations Manual.

Initial Fees. The franchise agreement will define the initial fees to be paid by the franchisee to the franchisor. The most common initial fee is the initial 'franchise fee' — the primary fee paid by the franchisee at the time of signing the franchise agreement. Other initial fees may include upfront software license fees and minimum startup inventory requirements.

Ongoing/Recurring Fees. The franchise agreement will define the ongoing fees the franchisee must pay to the franchisor and how they are calculated. The most common ongoing fee is the royalty fee, which is typically charged as a monthly or weekly fee paid by the franchisee to the franchisor. Royalties are calculated based on a fixed percentage (the royalty rate) of the franchisee's ongoing monthly or weekly gross sales, or a royalty might be based on a fixed dollar amount or other structure defined in the franchise agreement.

Marketing Fees and Marketing Obligations. The franchise agreement will mandate and define whether or not the franchisee is required to pay any marketing fees to the franchisor. The franchise agreement will establish whether or not a franchisee must contribute to a "brand development fund" and other obligations which the franchisee must satisfy regarding the franchisee's local marketing efforts.

Restrictive Covenants and Non-Competes. To protect the confidentiality of a franchise system and to prevent franchisees from establishing competing businesses, the franchise agreement will include in-term and post-termination restrictive covenants.

The "in-term" restrictive covenants will typically prohibit the franchisee from establishing, operating, or participating in any competing business during the term of the franchise agreement.

The "post-termination" restrictive covenants apply when the franchise agreement is terminated and will prohibit the franchisee from establishing, operating, or participating in any competing business for a designated time period that accrues following the date that the franchise agreement was terminated.

Legal Rights and Jurisdiction. The franchise agreement will define the state law (typically the law of the state where the Franchisor's corporate headquarters are located) that will govern the interpretation of the franchise agreement in cases of dispute. The franchise agreement will also define the state courts, federal courts, or arbitrating entity that will possess exclusive jurisdiction should a dispute arise between the franchisor and franchisee.

Your Franchise Agreements are negotiable. They are negotiable providing that the negotiated changes are based on a request of the franchisee and provide the franchisee with more favorable terms and rights, but not any less favorable terms or rights. While franchise agreements might be modified to gain a crucial franchisee or to respond to unique local circumstances, the modifications are most commonly of a limited nature. This allows franchisors some uniformity within their franchise systems. Do not negotiate your initial franchise fees and royalty obligations, as these are vital structural elements of your business.

Franchise Attorney Review & State Registrations

You have come this far and now you put all of your documents from the written business plan to the Franchise Agreement to the test — you have an experienced franchise attorney review it all. An attorney reviews all documents for each individual franchisee. Doing the heavy lifting and preliminary writing yourself will have saved you anywhere from $5,000 to $20,000 or more.

This attorney review and updating of the FDD can take anywhere between 1-4 weeks. Once the lawyers bless the documents, you are ready to develop your strategy on when and where to register your franchise opportunity.

Not all states are created equal or equally favorable with regard to franchising. Let's look at that now, and help you develop a strategy as to which state(s) you will register your franchise in.

FRANCHISE REGISTRATION STATES & FILING FEES

There are three primary franchise state registration types (and this could change at any time, so please refer to each state's current rules and regulations). The three primary types of franchise state registrations are as follows:

1)   Non-Registration States = Just need the Franchise Disclosure Document (FDD)

2) Filing States = Just file and pay a fee, no additional approval

3) Franchise Registration States = Just require filing, fee, and approval by state

Non-Registration States

The following **28** states do not require filing or registration to be able to sell franchises in the state. They only require that the franchisor follow the FTC guidelines and have an approved FDD.

Alabama	Kansas	Ohio
Alaska	Louisiana	Oklahoma
Arizona	Massachusetts	Oregon
Arkansas	Mississippi	Pennsylvania
Colorado	Missouri	Tennessee
Delaware	Montana	Vermont
District of Columbia	Nevada	West Virginia
Georgia	New Hampshire	Wyoming
Idaho	New Jersey	
Iowa	New Mexico	

Filing States:

These **9** states are 'filing states' that require the franchisor to file and pay a fee. They do not require the franchisor to submit documents and seek approval to sell franchises, like a registration state.

Connecticut is a franchise filing state and has a fee of $400.

Florida is a franchise filing state and has a fee of $100.

Kentucky is a franchise filing state and has a fee of $0.

Maine is a franchise filing state and has a fee of $25.

Nebraska is a franchise filing state and has a fee of $100.

North Carolina is a franchise filing state and has a fee of $250.

South Carolina is a franchise filing state and has a fee of $100.

Texas is a franchise filing state and has a fee of $25.

Utah is a franchise filing state and has a fee of $100.

Franchise Registration States:

These **13** states require registration and approval of Franchise Disclosure Document prior to selling in or from the state. These fees can and may change depending on the state regulators.

California Franchise Division Department of Corporations

1515 K Street, Suite 200 Sacramento, CA 95814

Franchise Registration Fee California $675

Hawaii Commissioner of Securities Department of Commerce and Consumer Affairs Business Registration Division Securities Compliance Branch

335 Merchant Street, Room 203, Honolulu, HA 96813

Franchise Registration Fee Hawaii $125

Illinois Franchise Division Office of Attorney General

500 South Second Street

Franchise Registration Fee Illinois $500

Indiana Franchise Division Office of Secretary of State

302 W. Washington St., Rm. E111 Indianapolis, IN 46204

Franchise Registration Fee Indiana $500

Maryland Office of the Attorney General Division of Securities

200 St Paul Place Baltimore, Maryland 21202-2020

Franchise Registration Fee Maryland $500

Michigan Consumer Protection Division Franchise Section

P.O. Box 30213 Lansing, MI 48909

Franchise Registration Fee Michigan $250

Minnesota Department of Commerce

85 7th Place East, Suite 500 St. Paul, MN 55101-2198

Franchise Registration Fee Minnesota $400

North Dakota Franchise Division Office of Securities Commission

600 East Boulevard – 5th Floor Bismarck, ND 58505

Franchise Registration Fee North Dakota $250

New York Franchise & Securities Division State Department of Law

120 Broadway 23rd Floor New York, NY 10271

Franchise Registration Fee New York $750

Rhode Island Franchise Office Division of Securities John O. Pastore Office Complex

1511 Pontiac Avenue, Bldg. 69-1 Cranston, RI 02910

Registration Fee Rhode Island $500

South Dakota Department of Revenue and Regulation Division of Securities

445 East Capitol Ave. Pierre, SD 57501

Registration Fee South Dakota $250

Virginia State Corporation Commission Division of Securities and Retail Franchising

1300 E. Main St. 9th Floor Richmond, VA 23219

Registration Fee Virginia $500

Washington (State) The Department of Financial Institutions Securities Division

P.O. Box 9033 Olympia, WA 98507-9033

Registration Fee Washington $600

Wisconsin Department of Financial Institutions Division of Securities

345 West Washington Ave., 4th Floor Madison, WI 53703

Registration Fee Wisconsin $400

FDD Renewal & Updates

Remember we said the FDD — the Franchise Disclosure Document — must be renewed annually? That is your opportunity to make modifications to it that might have become necessary due to your growth.

Under the Federal Franchise Rule, your FDD automatically expires 120 days after the end of your fiscal year (which is April 30th if you operate on a fiscal calendar year).

When your FDD expires, you must stop selling franchises. You must also evaluate when your FDD registrations and filings expire and require renewal at the state level.

NOTE: You will not need to rewrite the whole FDD from scratch, but you will need to update the points or the information so that it is accurate when you submit it for renewal.

Below is a chart listing the FDD registration, filing, and renewal requirements on a state-by-state basis, including FDD expiration dates:

Source: https://www.franchiselawsolutions.com/franchising/when-does-your-fdd-registration-expire/

State	Registration or Filing State	State Expiration Dates
California	Registration	Annual registration required. Expires 110 days after your fiscal year end.
Connecticut	Registration / Exemption	If you have a federally registered trademark, then one-time exemption filing that does not expire. If you do not have a federally registered trademark then you must register annually. Registration expires 1 year from registration effective date.
Florida	Filing	Annual filing required. Expires 1 year from filing effective date.
Hawaii	Registration	Annual registration required. Expires 90 days after your fiscal year end.
Illinois	Registration	Annual registration required. Expires 120 days after your fiscal year end.
Indiana	Registration	Annual registration required. Expires 1 year from registration effective date.
Kentucky	Filing	One time filing only; no expiration.
Maine	Filing / Exemption	If you have a federally registered trademark, then no filing required. If you do not have a federally registered trademark then filing required. Filing expires 1 year from filing effective date.
Maryland	Registration	Annual registration required. Expires 1 year from registration effective date.
Michigan	Registration	Annual notice filing required. Expires 1 year from notice filing date.
Minnesota	Registration	Annual registration required. Expires 120 days after your fiscal year end.
Nebraska	Filing	One time filing; no expiration.
New York	Registration	Annual registration required. Expires 120 days after your fiscal year end.
North Dakota	Registration	Annual registration required. Expires 120 days after your fiscal year end.
Rhode Island	Registration	Annual registration required. Expires 1 year from registration date; must submit renewal 30 days prior to expiration.
South Carolina	Filing / Exemption	One time filing if you have a registered trademark.

State	Registration or Filing State	State Expiration Dates
South Dakota	Filing	Annual filing required. Expires 1 year from filing effective date.
Texas	Filing	One time filing; no expiration.
Utah	Filing	Annual Filing is required. Expires 1 year from filing effective date.
Virginia	Registration	Annual registration required. Expires 1 year from registration effective date.
Washington	Registration	Annual registration required. Expires 1 year from registration effective date.
Wisconsin	Registration	Annual registration required. Expires 1 year from registration effective date.

RESOLVING CONFLICTS BETWEEN STATE AND FEDERAL RULE RENEWAL REQUIREMENTS

Many times, a conflict exists between the date by which your FDD must be updated under the federal franchise rule and the date that your state registrations and filings must be updated.

Let's say your franchise company operates on a fiscal calendar year basis and your most recent state registration occurred on October 1st. Under the federal 120-day rule, your FDD will expire on April 30th — even though under your state's law your registration lasts for one year and will remain effective until October 1st. As of April 30th, your FDD will have expired nonetheless and you must stop selling franchises in Virginia on April 30th.

To avoid annual headaches and operating illegally, prior to April 30th on the first year of your franchisor operations, the appropriate course of action is to file for FDD registration renewal with the state. At the time of this filing, you could request that the state changes the effective date of your registrations so that it is in sync with the federal 120-day requirement.

Anytime there is a significant material change in the information disclosed in your FDD, you must update your FDD *within the quarter*. Once updated, you will be required to update your state registrations through a post-effective amendment process.

What is a 'material change'? If a change relates to facts or information that would influence the decision-making process of a reasonable franchisee, then you should consider such a change as 'material' and make the FDD update. Changes in information related to your FDD's Item 19 *'Financial Performance Representations'* must be made immediately given their crucial part in franchisee decision-making.

Operations

Today's businesses, as you already know from running a successful one, have many moving parts that we call 'operations'. Let's look at the primary moving parts of a business in this Phase.

The usual ones include, but are not limited to:

- Software/hardware is an ever-present aspect of running the business.

- Supply chain (your vendors) is a crucial moving part — one missed shipment or out-of-stock part and you could be in trouble.

- Staff (personnel or human resources), both on-site and remote, is a vital part of operations all about delivering your service or product.

- Customer service is about staff with customer-facing roles but also about call centers, email responsiveness, and other tools.

- Marketing, promotion, and advertising is multi-media and multi-platform; it demands daily attention.

- Accountancy and tax matters demand excellent record keeping.

All of the moving parts of your business were documented in your business plan, and now is the time to convert that documentation into manuals for your franchisees and their staff to learn from and continuously consult. Instead of one all-inclusive manual, franchisees are usually provided with a series of manuals.

A WELL-KNOWN BRAND

Anytime Fitness wants to get your franchise running and keep your franchise fit. I like this franchisor story, not so much because it is unique, but because of the clarity of support they provide to franchisees.

Part of what will draw franchise candidates to you is the quality of information — and how clear it is — available on your website and, when they request it, in your additional detailed literature. When you don't mask the costs, franchisees are happier. When you clearly state in the training what needs doing and how on a daily basis, your franchisees are comforted.

Go to Anytime Fitness's franchisee website to get an idea of a clear map for the franchise candidate. Then apply how they have done it to your own business concept (because Anytime's approach, though totally clear, may not be exactly for you).

Operational success begins with the franchisee possessing clear, complete, and accurate information from you. You've 'been there, done that' and the franchisee expects you to share that experience upfront.

Franchisor & Franchisee Software

Software applications are the operating tools for all businesses today. I can't think of any business that does not employ software for several — if not most — functions.

As the franchisor, computer-based systems are likely to be the backbone of your data collection, data storage, and data analysis capabilities. Part of the assurance that you make to franchisees is that your locations' systems and software are fully functioning and able to handle franchisees' business transactions with ease.

This is going to take some research on your end, and typically the system you are using now to run your business may not be the right system for all of your franchisees to use. If you have pieced together a software program or used your cousin's Microsoft Office serial numbers, that's obviously not going to work for your franchisees. Having your business email as a Gmail account or other free web-based account isn't going to cut it either.

There are several well-known platforms for franchisors to help manage the day-to-day operations of being a franchisor and working with franchisees. The one I have the most experience with is FranConnect (www.franconnect.com), and it is by far the largest player in the franchisor software space. However, they focus heavily on large enterprise clients with hundreds and thousands of locations, so it may be overkill for 95% of most small/brand-new franchisors like yourself.

Here are three others to consider:

- Naranga: https://naranga.com/
- Franchise Soft: https://franchisesoft.com/
- FRM Solutions: https://www.frmsolutions.com/

To get started, you will need to do a complete audit of all your day-to-day software — all mobile apps and software you use to run your business — to identify any holes or problems you would have as a franchisor. Most industries we work with have very well-developed Point of Sale (POS) systems with great training and resources available.

For example, if you're in the food, home services, real estate, fitness, hotel, or retail sectors, there are hundreds of great platforms to use. But one of the brands I've worked with was a business brokerage franchise, and there were no software platforms available for business brokers. So after five years of working and trying to use Salesforce's CRM product without success, they built their own in-house (proprietary) platform.

For this audit, it may be more efficient to hire an IT consultant.

About IT (Information Technologies) consultants: ask if they work with and already have a franchisor program in place. Many of them do have enterprise-level accounts and representatives that can help guide you through the A to Z of what's necessary for multi-location functionality and processes. If they do, then they will know the questions to ask you about your business operations, and the transactions that you perform and advise on software.

If the IT company you are currently using has never worked with a franchisor and doesn't have a multi-location enterprise level plan, you are going to have to switch providers. You simply can't survive without this franchise-wide functionality and reporting.

With that said, here below is a checklist of items to get a solidly experienced IT consultant to audit and review in relation to your purposes.

Your Current Software/POS:

I've had clients gloss over this piece. They allowed their first five franchisees to choose the software they wanted to have, instead of requiring one enterprise level system. Then 30 days in, they realized they had no access to their sales or revenue, and most importantly, no way to verify and collect royalties. They have to go one-by-one and ask each location for reporting on a monthly basis now.

Get a franchise-wide Point of Sale system.

Customer Relationship Management (CRM) Software:

CRM software is a multifaceted tool. You can store customer and prospect contact information, accounts, leads, and sales opportunities in one central location — ideally in the cloud so the information is accessible by many, in real time. It allows you to prepare and schedule email blasts, and more. A CRM gives everyone across the business, including sales, customer service, marketing, and business development, offering a better way to access and manage the customer relationship and interactions you have on a daily or periodic basis. Most CRM packages are expandable (aka scalable), so that it grows with your franchise business.

Many modern POS systems have some basic level CRM system built in, but very few are adequate at scale. Before going down this rabbit hole, ask your IT consultant about POS providers and CRM providers that can be directly integrated. You will start to hear scary words like API being thrown around, but don't worry about all that for now; just focus on ensuring you have a CRM tool that works flawlessly with your POS system.

Windows & PC vs Apple & Mac

I'm very biased here, but my overall opinion is valid. I was Avionic Electronic Engineer in the Air Force, and I've personally built almost every computer I've owned. For 90% of franchisors, Windows-based products that run on PC hardware for mass scale is the better way to go. You simply have many more options, vendors, and far better pricing for the same functional items than you do with Apple-based products.

If you are in education, advertising (or other graphics-intensive field), or music businesses — Apple has focused heavily on the needs of these industries, and might be the way to go (and these types of franchises are relatively rare, so my PC/Windows recommendation holds).

Another important reason is that most of your franchisees probably already used PC and Office products in their previous corporate roles. In my observations, 90% of franchisees will be coming out of corporate America jobs, where they are probably already using a Windows-based platform and are familiar with Microsoft products from daily use.

Email Provider

Never allow franchisees to use personal, free web-based accounts such as Gmail or Yahoo for their business. You need to make sure all your email accounts are on one franchise-wide, 'enterprise' platform (like your POS system — that is, you chose it and they are obligated to use it). Do not let each franchisee use a different system.

I recommend only considering two service providers: "G-Suite" by Google and "Office 365" by Microsoft to manage all of your franchisor and franchisee emails. Without a doubt, I prefer "Office 365" by Microsoft as the product to use to manage your email accounts and other tech items with your franchisees and at the corporate level. I just find the Office 365 platform to be more professional in its look and feel. Again, most franchisee candidates natively understand how to use Microsoft products.

Email Marketing

Now that you have a POS & CRM system, you need to look at an email marketing system. It might already be integrated into your CRM, so ask.

An email marketing system/platform is one where you can store your database of names, write emails (or a series of emails for an email blast), and schedule them to be sent to a certain segment of your list, or the entire list, on a given future date.

You need an effective, and most importantly, trackable method for you and your franchisees to communicate with your customers, so this choice is important for your peace of mind. There are dozens of email marketing platforms including MailChimp, ACTIVE Campaign, and Constant Contact. I recommend using Constant Contact (https://www.constantcontact.com/partners/franchise). Constant Contact has a built-in franchisor program that is currently the best in the industry.

Accounting Software

It is vitally important that you get your franchisees properly set up from Day One with seamlessly automated accounting software — and get them trained on using it. Consult your IT person again, as well as the company producing the chosen accounting software, about training modules or free classes.

If not trained immediately and effectively, a few months down the road, a panicky franchisee will be asking for help — or when you ask to see their P&L, they will say "I don't have one."

I only recommend going with one of the big names in accounting software as they are all robust and have great training and service. I recommend reviewing QuickBooks and Xero. Between the two, I recommend QuickBooks (by Intuit, https://quickbooks.intuit.com/franchise/). Why? QuickBooks has finally launched a franchise program.

You will also want to confirm with your POS/CRM provider that they work with QuickBooks. 99% do but be sure to ask.

Training is easy with a QuickBooks selection: there are thousands of local, national, and international QuickBooks experts to help you get everything setup properly. Also, all CPAs and bookkeepers know and understand how to use QuickBooks data.

This should cover the basic operational software tools for now — and these should get you very far down the road, helping to prevent stress and confusion in working with your franchisees.

Franchisee Locations & Approved Vendors

Now we have to look at everything needed for starting your franchisees' own businesses — specifically, building your franchisees' commercial spaces out from scratch.

Think about the franchises you have frequented. The 'look' and 'feel' of the spaces are always identical from location to location — even across states and into foreign countries (a McDonald's in Paris France or in New York City is instantly identifiable to anyone who has seen just one McDonald's location, say, in Tokyo, Japan). That is your goal here, as you prepare this part of your plan.

Keep in mind, it will be impossible to enforce exact aspects at every location. Many cities or developments have strict codes on signage, colors, material used, or other aspects they require. Even the large mega brands like McDonald's allow for unique aspects and design (i.e.: locations built to resemble a Happy Meal box). There are also variations within that design that can make a difference. As you may have noticed most Chick-fil-A's are stand-alone buildings (key word 'most'). They also allow for non-traditional locations inside malls, airports, and other locations. Some locations have playgrounds, and some don't. Just a few items to consider when sourcing your vendors to help scale your franchise.

Please keep in mind that if you yourself built and outfitted your original business premises on a shoestring budget — went to garage sales, placed Facebook and Craigslist ads to get your business equipment and furnishings, and all that needed labor — that will not work for a franchisee. You need to give your franchisees a solid plan and a pre-packaged list of resources, vendors, suppliers, and such to help them build out their chosen commercial space.

You may have to build this from scratch, outlining a replicable program to open up a new location with the proper tools and resources that you have fully detailed and negotiated. I work with dozens of outside construction, design, and build-out vendors — and so will you as a franchisor wanting to get it all right.

You have to have a plan in place with each to get your locations 1) looking like your original concept and brand (site and space location and its buildout and equipping) and 2) up and running smoothly.

You can count on needing anywhere from 5 to 25 vendors to open up each location, since they are all specialists and no single one does it all.

For example, you might have four furniture vendors, two IT companies, along with one for each of the following: construction, project management, marketing, PR, coffee, cleaning, and security. Many of them will pay rebates back to you as well (a sort of finder's fee for bringing them the business), and they may even agree upfront to sponsor events that you are running. Each of these vendors are sourced by you, and each one has a separate MSA (Master Service Agreement) negotiated, signed, and kept active.

There is an easy button for this part of the program, and it is called 'outsourcing'. You can outsource the entire process to a project and development management service company. There are retail space designers, outfitters who bring in the entire crew to do everything from gutting the space to furnishing it for opening day. This can be very expensive, and the cost needs to be disclosed if you add this. Alternatively, you may opt to handle it all yourself and make a profit on marking up items. There is no real right or wrong here, as long as it is done properly, is repeatable for you, and is fully disclosed to your franchisees. What you cannot do is not have a plan on where, when, and how much it will cost for your franchisee to start a complete turnkey variation of your business model.

WHAT IS INVOLVED?

Retail and commercial space remodels are overseen by project and development advisors who understand design and construction. Project managers hire and manage, schedule, and monitor construction teams and budgets.

The first step will be for you, the franchisor, to hire such pros to draw up the design, layout, furnishings, equipment, and furniture your business is using in its original location. That is the concept the model franchisees will be cloning.

If you, the franchisor, choose to hire one project management company to oversee the build out of each future franchisee location, that company must be able to travel to those franchisee locations with crews that do the work. Below I list, in no particular order. some of the traditional services offered by commercial build-out firms.

Single-Site Project Management

- Site Selection and Due Diligence

- Capital and Tenant Fit-out

- Building Repositioning and Modernization

- Design and Construction Management

- Furniture, Fixtures, and Equipment (FF&E) Management

- Program Management

Multi-Site Project Delivery

- Centralized Project Controls and Reporting

- Cost Management and Benchmarking

- Process and Standards Development

- Development Advisory and Management

Build-to-Suit

- Adaptive Re-use

- Land Planning and Feasibility Analysis

- RFP Development
- Financing Strategies

Additional Services

- Strategic Planning
- Property Condition Assessments
- Space and Occupancy Planning
- Relocation and Logistics Management
- Sustainability

Operations Manuals

Congrats for starting from scratch to decide whether franchising is your path to grow and also for making it to this point! It is a lot to take in, but most of your 'heavy lifting' is done before the first franchisee is identified and starts the work to open his or her door.

If you enter a franchised business, and then a while later go into the same franchise in a different town, you will clearly notice that both locations look, sound, serve, and sell like clones of each other. And that is the point! It is because of the build-out and design I presented in the prior section. But there is more. It is about what the staff does — and how.

You can do this templated or cloned operating only with a master guidebook that each franchisee and location manager follows to the letter. This will be your Franchise Operations Manual. You need to ensure it is accurate, up to date, easy to read and find answers within, and properly represents your business.

The Operations Manual should identify each franchisee's contractual obligations to you and the complete details regarding how you expect them to fulfil these obligations. The Manual answers all their operational 'how-to-do-it' questions and usually in more detail than an online FAQ would be able to deliver.

When manuals are properly produced as step-by-step how-to guides, your franchisees bother you less because they have a go-to resource. They are more profitable and become promoters of your franchise. And your business looks and sounds and feels like your own business — from one location to all the others.

Because the Operations Manual contains confidential information that a franchisor shares with its franchisees, the Operations Manual is not disclosed in the FDD. However, the FDD <u>must</u> disclose the number of pages and table of contents to the Operations Manual.

STARTUP FRANCHISORS AND THE OPERATIONS MANUAL

Within your FDD and Franchise Agreement there will be numerous references to your "confidential Operations Manual". Your FDD and Franchise Agreement will state that your franchisees are legally required to follow the systems and procedures you disclose in the Operations Manual and that you may, in the future, modify this from time to time.

Thus, as a startup franchisor, your Operations Manual will serve an important business and legal role in your franchise system. It is your business's source of information to providing consistent service, consistent operations, clear procedures — and thus serves as a training tool for initial and later staff that are hired and trained by the franchisee.

With a well-designed, detailed, and easy-to-reference Ops Manual, your franchisees will be comforted, and you will be better assured of 100% quality control (assurance that your concept is replicated and protected).

WHO PREPARES THE OPERATIONS MANUAL?

Although you may never write a word of it yourself as the business owner, you need to be intimately involved with the preparation of the Operations Manual. After all, who knows the business you created better than you?

Whether you prepare your Operations Manual yourself or work with an outside franchise development team, your direct participation will be critical because your Operations Manual needs to reflect your business and your systems. When it comes to developing your Operations Manual, it is critical that you avoid generic content, and instead get to the heart of what your business is all about and how franchisees can duplicate your brand and success.

A great way to start is to get each of your current staff to write up 1) their own job description and 2) the step-by-step of how they do the various parts/tasks of their job. Give them plenty of paid work time to do this and you'll have a terrific headstart on a complete Manual. Your team will also have saved you consulting fees by getting this far.

Topics Included in Your Operations Manual

- Introduce your new franchisee to your corporate management team, your brand, and your mission as a business.

- Inform and educate your franchisees about 1) what business values you hold as paramount, 2) how your franchise system operates, 3) your relationship with them, and 4) your collective relationship with exclusive manufacturers and the supplies you require that they use.

- Inform and educate your franchisees about the steps involved in building-out and establishing their franchised outlet.

- Inform and educate your franchisees about how to conduct the day-to-day operations of the franchised business.

- Inform and educate your franchisees about their administrative and reporting obligations.

- Inform your franchisees about the confidentiality of the Operations Manual.

Information Goal 1: The Role of the Operations Manual

Your first goal is to inform and educate the franchisee and his or her staff about the business they're in, how it operates, the responsibilities and tasks of each employee in the business, and how we treat our customers with our walk and our talk.

Information Goal 2: Your Story and Mission

It is here that your Operations Manual should convey 'your story'. Give background to how your business got started. Tell the story of your business evolution so that franchisees become familiar with the business they are about to invest in. Tell the story of your business concept, your brand, your value to customers, and what it is that keeps them coming back to you.

Information Goal 3: What the Business Does and How It Does It

Information and education about the products and services you bring to your targeted consumers.

- How do you reach your consumers with information about your business?

- How do you communicate with your consumers (direct advertising, digital presence, direct networking, and front line time with clients through surveys or face-to-face conversation, etc.)?

- How do you develop, prepare, and provide your products or services to customers?

- Why do you price the way you do?

- Who are the business's preferential vendors and suppliers?

- What sort of equipment — hardware software and other tools — are provided to employees to perform their work?

- How do franchisees report revenues, other performance data, and feedback to the franchisor?

Information Goal 4: Marketing and Business Development

This is about the franchisee's obligation to market and develop the business.

This is a critical section since, much more often than not, successful franchisees are not the ones who are working 'in the business'; i.e.: providing the service or selling product. The successful ones are rather those continuously working to market, promote, and manage the franchise business.

This section of the manual teaches franchisees to work 'on their franchised business' not 'in their franchised business'. Topics may include the following:

- The right mindset for success

- Approved marketing strategies

- The role of direct mail

- The role of print media

- Use of our website

- Use of social media

- Email marketing

- Newsletters

- Use of Groupon and similar "pre-sale discount" sites

- Using CRM & POS (customer relationship management; point of sale) systems

Information Goal 5: Approved Products, Suppliers, and Providers

Details about establishing their franchised business, including details and lists relating to issues such as approved build-out plans, requirements and restrictions for signage, and lists of approved suppliers.

Details about operating their franchised business such as approved recipes and step-by-step instructions for services and/or products, scripts for answering phone calls, scripts for responding to emails, how to request approval of other vendors, etc.

Will your Operations Manual be a carbon copy of that other franchise's manual? No, you will naturally adapt information to your business and your industry.

It is important to understand that your Operations Manual is a dynamic tool that will be adjusted over time — modified, supplemented. Developing the right Operations Manual will take you a long way toward establishing a solid foundation with your franchisees and maintaining control over your franchise system.

Launch

At this point, you are ready to open the door to growth as a franchisor! You have completed your planning. Your legal documents are ready and filed. Your Operations and Training Manuals are complete.

You are ready to do the marketing, selling, and training that will open up new franchise locations with franchisees.

This phase is where things get fun and scary at the same time. You are ready to tell the world that you have a great franchise opportunity. This phase is about marketing — sharing the fact that you now franchise your concept and attracting qualified candidates to buy a franchise.

Marketing leads to the sale of a franchise to one or more candidates.

The sale leads to training, which in turn leads to finding and securing the best new location for the franchisee and building it out.

You will need to line up some financing options to help your franchisees with capital to get started with the launch and early months of their new business.

You will need to devote personal time to each new franchisee to ensure not only their success, but your own — as this following story helps to illustrate.

A WELL-KNOWN BRAND

A higher percentage of Americans than almost anywhere else in the world are homeowners. And naturally (as every homeowner knows) repairs, upkeep, and maintenance, not to mention remodeling to stay relevant and to keep the value of the house high, are a never-ending chore.

That is why our country is so rich in mega-hardware stores for the do-it-yourselfer, and equally rich in home improvement services and craft businesses for those who cannot do it themselves.

This is why I like this story about Budget Blinds. It is a 1,000-location+ franchisor that represents about 30% of outlets in the franchised home decor category, making it the largest player in the space by far.

It's also a good deal for first-time franchisees. Why? Because Budget Blinds has made a reputation for itself by providing *loads of training* to their franchisees. They understand the ins-and-outs of operations, and how important *ongoing support* can be to making that new customer happy…and creating referrals for new business down the road.

The franchisor has got a solid, reputable, recognized brand. The franchisees have limited turnover — meaning that they are so happy and doing so well in the business that they stay with Budget Blinds at a far higher rate than other franchisees with other franchisors.

Budget Blinds has understood that 'the devil is in the details' and they have outstanding Operations Manuals, Franchisee and Staff Training Programs, and an ongoing support system. So should you.

Franchise Sales & Marketing

Congratulations, you are now a fully functioning franchisor and ready to start down the path of finding your first franchisee.

Clearly understand this — not all franchisee leads and sources are created equal. Understand, too, that there is a such thing as a standardized sales process. But whichever sales process you use, you must follow its steps systematically.

Set a marketing budget, and put the proper people, systems, and processes into place to help automate parts of your franchise sales. Follow your IT consultant's best advice on building a franchise sales website, and, finally, outline a budget and your sales goals for your first 12 months as franchisor.

Additionally, you should seriously consider consulting a marketing professional experienced in *generating qualified leads*. Do this even if you never needed to in your original business. You might pay the marketing person or agency on a monthly retainer plan and agree that they manage all your online/offline advertising, social media, and the like. Not all business owners are marketers, and that is why contracting the work out is a perfect remedy.

WHAT IS YOUR SALES GOAL FOR YEAR ONE?

First things first! If you followed our business planning process, you should have already written down a franchise sales goal for the first year. Let's say that goal is five new or non-friend, non-family, non-customer new franchisees for the first year.

On a side note, we have worked with clients who sold 100 franchises in the first 12 months. Realistically, five to ten would be more typical.

Food for thought: If your annual goal were five signatures on those FAs, and 13 franchisee candidates made the cut — would your personnel, your systems, and...your nerves...be ready for nearly triple that number? We've heard of servers 'crashing'. We don't want your business to do so!

So if your year-one sales goal is five franchisees, how many leads do you think you will need to generate to sell that many franchises? Or stated differently, what would you expect your closing percentage to be? Many of our clients have said they have a goal of closing 10% to 20% of the leads that they generate. Well, that is a great goal if you were selling low mileage Ferraris, but completely unrealistic when it comes to selling franchises to the general franchise buyer.

Generally speaking, franchise sales closing rates tend to be 1% to 2% of all leads in. That is, most franchisors, large and small, close on average 1 to 2 people out of every 100 leads they receive. Every now and then a brand goes viral and starts selling itself but prepare sales goals appropriately to accomplish that goal.

As a brand-new franchisor, plan on a 0.5-1% closing ratio for your first year, while you are still learning about the industry and getting comfortable in the space and your new role.

START WITH LEAD GENERATION

The obvious place to start to get the word out is literally that way — by word-of-mouth. Tell people that you are now a franchisor. Tell your current customer/client database and talk with your own professional and community networks. Ask them to tell the people they know — it will get some 'buzz' going.

Many of my new startup franchisors end up getting their first franchisee or two right from their current sphere of influence. With that said, it is great to land a couple of franchisees from your database, but you are probably not going to accomplish your first-year sales goals with just that approach.

Using other media, I recommend that you additionally start advertising in your store, on your website, and spread the word on your social media accounts. I never recommend just banking on your brand going viral and selling itself.

If you have a goal of selling 5 franchises your first year, we estimate you will need to generate 500 to 1,000 new prospects/leads over the first year to hit that sales goal. This would be 42 to 85 new leads per month. Obviously then, beyond walk-in clients, you need to have a marketing plan and budget to be able to support generating a steady flow of qualified leads for your opportunity.

How much money do you need to spend monthly to generate those 42 to 85 qualified leads per month — or to achieve 1,000 leads that year? In my observations of many franchisors, I have concluded that your average lead cost is right at $60, blending all of your marketing techniques together. So we would estimate you need to have $2,500 to $5,000 per month to invest into franchise sales lead generation.

We have four primary sources for franchise sales lead generation listed below in the order of cost and quality. They are so equal in their power to build your franchise that you must not neglect any of them.

4 Sources of Franchise Sales Lead Generation:*

- Internet = 30% of leads come from 3rd party franchise portal leads

- Brand = 30% of leads come from our own franchise website and store locations

- Brokers = 20% of leads come from franchise consultants and brokers

- Tradeshows = 20% of leads come from Franchise Trade Shows

*See Resource List at end of the book

FRANCHISE SALES SCRIPTS, WEBSITE, & MARKETING BROCHURE

You should be able to have your entire sales pitch down to one page, and we also recommend developing a separate franchising website from your corporate business website. In addition, many people still like reviewing material, so we recommend creating a PDF brochure or document of some type to provide to prospects for them to review.

FRANCHISE SALES SOFTWARE

If you are generating 40-90+ leads per month, you are going to need a system and process to properly handle, maintain, and respond to those 500 to 1,000 requests over the year. You don't want to lose a single lead because your processes and systems don't work. Every lead closed is worth tens of thousands of dollars in future fees and royalties! At my company, United Franchise Group, we use FranConnect (our choice of CRM, or Customer Relationship Management software tool) to manage over *40,000 inquiries per year* — and not one name or number has ever been lost. Our system has never crashed.

Unless you have experience with setting up CRM systems, hire an experienced contractor (your IT consultant can recommend a qualified one).

FRANCHISE SALES PROCESS

Now that you are generating leads and talking with potential prospects, you need to understand that there is a process to selling franchises, much like there is a process to buying or selling a home. Let's simplify the process!

The franchise sales process can be broken down into 7 simple steps:

- **Initial Screening** = 3-5-minute call to go over the basic information about your franchise opportunity. Highlighting what your business does, what makes you different, the investment needed, and booking a follow-up appointment which should be either a face-to-face meeting if possible or a webinar.

- **Meeting or Webinar** = Typically, this is a 60-minute meeting to discuss in more detail the franchise opportunity and get to know the prospect better. I recommend trying to do some research via LinkedIn or other online sources about the prospect before this call.

- **Application** = If the prospect is still interested and you are still interested in them, at this point we ask them to complete a Franchise Application for review.

- **FDD Review** = After receiving the application, we send the prospect the FDD to review, and receive back the receipt acknowledging they received it (14-day holding period required by law).

- **Discovery Day** = Book this time to have the prospect come and spend the day with you to learn more about your franchise opportunity. Some franchisors pay for the prospect to attend and some do not; the choice is yours.

- **Deposit** = If the prospect is still interested after visiting, we collect a fully refundable deposit, typically $5,500, to start putting together the franchise agreement and taking their territory off the market (The 14-day waiting period after FDD applies).

- **Closing** = Sign the Franchise Agreement. Collect the remaining balance of the franchise fee.

That is the full process of selling your first franchise.

At this point, I just want to briefly touch on one more point almost guaranteed to come up if you grow your business into a large multi-location franchise organization.

FRANCHISE RESALES

Again, just like buying and selling a home, people will need to exit their franchise. At some point, people decide to do something different. Perhaps family or health issues decide for them. Sometimes people sell their franchise because they have made their nut and are cashing out and moving on. Other times they sell their franchise because they are not making the money they had hoped for or are otherwise unhappy with the 'fit' of the business to their personality.

Any way it comes to you, it is important that you have a plan and understand the franchise resale process.

Your FDD will state the *transfer fee* that is required, and just know that the process is essentially the same for a resale as it is for a new franchise set-up. The only differences are 1) there are really three agreements being signed and 2) the new franchisee does not have to build out a store since they take one over.

In a resale, there is a buy/sell agreement between the current franchisee and the new franchisee buying the existing business. Then there is a new franchise agreement being signed by the new franchisee. Finally, once funded, there is a general release for the old franchisee, releasing them from their obligations of the franchise agreement.

At this stage, that is all you need to know about Franchise Sales and Marketing.

Again, I strongly suggest working with a competent and franchise-specific marketing company to help you achieve your sales and marketing goals.

Franchise Financing

This is a vital aspect of being a franchisor. It is a rare business that has a pile of ready cash to invest when they come to me asking how to franchise.

Imagine if you went to buy a car or a home and your salesperson didn't have a process in place to assist you with financing. The offer of mortgage financing or auto loans is a universal tool they use to close the deal.

Selling franchises is no different — you, too, want to 'close the deal' with a qualified franchise candidate. You can completely outsource this financing process from A-Z, as many other industries do.

More often than not, there are just three ways that franchisees finance their new franchise:

- **Self-Funded/Friends & Family** = They have the money in the bank from savings, profitable investments, or, if they have come to you from their salaried career, they may have a plush retirement account they are willing to dive into. If they are moving from another business ownership type, they may have sold that business for a profit and used the funds to launch this franchise.

You probably didn't know this, but you can use the money in your 401(k) to pay yourself and start a franchise. One of my preferred partners, *Benetrends,* offers a 401(k)/IRA Business Funding program. More details are here: https://www.benetrends.com/programs/business-funding-solutions/401-k-ira-business-financing.

- ■ **Franchisor Financing** = Maybe you yourself have the capital and capacity to lend money to your franchisees to start the business.

This is not very common, but when you are able to, it can make for an amazing opportunity. This is what *Chick-fil-A* does…need I say more?! You can see details about their model here: https://www.chick-fil-a.com/our-standards/independently-operated-and-connecting-with-customers.

- ■ **SBA Loan Funding** = Typically, at least two banks in your franchisee's area are going to be SBA lenders; they lend from $100,000 to $5 million. The beauty of these loans is what happens if the borrower defaults: you are liable for only a portion of the unrepaid loan amount, while the federal government covers or 'guarantees' the rest.

Go to www.sba.gov for general information and links to details. For the form and process, consult my friends and approved vendor at *Guidant Financial* here: https://www.guidantfinancial.com/blog/franchise-financing-sba-loans/.

Whether your franchisee seeks a traditional or an SBA loan from his or her banker, banks analyze the qualification criteria closely. They refer to it as the "5 C's" of SBA loans: Capital, Credit, Collateral, Capacity, and Character. If you are deep in such conversations with a franchise candidate, inform him of these five qualifying points and get the ball rolling in his head. If your candidates see you as an information source, it builds trust and gets them closer to signing on the bottom line!

Let's now examine that SBA financial terminology — both you and your franchisee will need to understand this in order to make sure they are 'loan-worthy'.

CAPITAL

Capital refers specifically to your equity injection or down payment. In other words, this is the amount of money you're putting down at the start of the loan to show your good faith toward paying it back.

For most SBA lenders, the down payment requirement will be between 20% (if you're buying an existing business or franchise location) to 30% (funding a brand-new businesses). It's important to note that opening a new franchise location is considered a 'new' business by lenders, so be prepared to pay that higher down payment.

Since the down payment is typically non-negotiable for banks, you may want to wait to apply for the loan until you're able to provide it. If saving to achieve 20–30% of your loan amount isn't an option for you, there are other ways to fulfil the down payment requirement, such as 401(k) business financing.

CREDIT

We have FICO (from 'Fair Isaac Corporation') scores as individuals and as businesses. They measure our creditworthiness. The higher the score, the better (theoretically) the creditworthiness.

Not only will lenders look for a FICO credit score of 690+, they'll make sure you don't have any recent bankruptcies or foreclosures and few (or zero) delinquent payments.

While it is possible to still qualify for an SBA loan with one of the above-listed negative factors, it should be far, far in your past and not a recent occurrence.

COLLATERAL

This is 'something of value pledged to the lender if the borrower defaults.'

Even though banks are guaranteed to be paid a certain percentage of an SBA loan in the event of your default, they typically ask you to put up personal property to secure the loan from their end. Homes are the most common form of collateral, but other types of real property or financial instruments are acceptable.

Property or valuables that you put up as collateral have a 'lien' attached to them. You won't be able to cash out or sell any such item until the lien is satisfied and lifted.

CAPACITY

Can you earn enough cash from the business to cover the bills, and also pay back your loan in monthly instalments? That is the question that 'capacity' seeks to answer.

Your current income, spouse's income, and projected future business income enter into the bank's calculations of your capacity to repay. For new franchisees, lenders will look for more income outside the business to offset any cash flow issues during the launch phase and first year of operations.

CHARACTER

This is about your resume, your business profile, your 'bio'. Does your past experience in the world of work show potential to succeed in this venture? Lenders want to ensure the numbers line up on paper, but they also want proof that you have a demonstrable past ability to run and manage a business.

Banks likewise review your personal history. Late child support payments, criminal convictions, and arrests are red flags for lenders.

MANAGING THE SBA LENDING PROCESS

SBA-guaranteed loans can take up to 90 days to process. If your franchise candidate needs such a loan to purchase a franchise, you may want to negotiate enough time into the purchase agreement to allow for loan processing.

With running any business or household, keeping your paperwork and records in order and handy is key to moving the process along quickly. You will be asked to provide lots of information, so be sure to keep photocopies of everything submitted.

Generally, franchise financing SBA loans are amortized over ten years (unless real estate is attached to the loan). The amortization period may be shorter, but the default length of the loan is ten years.

Rates change as the money markets and FICO scores and the general economy evolve, so an interest rate quoted to you six months ago may have dropped or risen by the time you come to take out the loan.

Franchisee Training

FRANCHISEE TRAINING SCHOOL

You will need a plan on how to properly support, train, and retrain your franchisees and their employees over the lifespan of their franchise business. Stability and success demand it.

Of all the tasks that befall you as a new franchisor, perhaps none are as important as training. Training keeps the people in every location doing the same things according to your original concept; it keeps them all preserving the culture, the brand, the look, the feel, and the tone of the business.

Understand this: You need trainer-facilitated sessions — simply asking everyone to 'read the manuals and sign here, please' is not training!

When is your next training school for new franchisees and their staff? Who is actually going to do the training?

As early as possible, you want to start looking at creating a fixed or recurring franchisee training schedule. The load can become heavy: if you sell 10 franchises in a short period of time and agree to two weeks of training each, that's 20 weeks of training if done back-to-back. Instead you might have franchisee training once a quarter at a set date and time. This way you can consolidate the training of multiple franchisee teams into the same period. Avoid the scheduling nightmare.

For consistent results, it is important to follow the training curriculum you created when making your FDD.

MANUALS ARE YOUR BRAND PROTECTION

Creating the Ops and Training Manuals may have seemed somewhat expensive. As stated earlier, doing the work yourself as much as possible saves you cash. The alternative of having inadequate brand protection may be much more costly. This whole training exercise and ongoing training for support purposes is an area in which it is generally unwise to cut corners. Like a poorly written Operations Manual, lack of training will at best tarnish your brand, and at worst may easily lead you into a courtroom.

The courtroom? Yes, and the first area of potential exposure occurs when you try to enforce system standards without this Operations Manual. Many standards are qualitative as opposed to quantitative, making things impossible to measure 'up to standard'. A specialist consultant will know how to formulate such standards in order to ensure clarity and transparency.

More costly litigation can come up when a consumer lawsuit tries to attach you, the franchisor, to one of your franchisee's actions. Generally speaking, the franchisee, as an independent contractor, is responsible for its own actions.

Making sure your Operations Manual literally 'says it all' is vital to protecting your business! The starting point and reference books for all training is the Operations Manual first, and the actual Training Manual second.

NEXT, THE DETAILED TRAINING PROGRAM

The Operations Manual is your franchisee's 'workbook' and reference during training, as they learns to operate the business in the prescribed way. The primary purpose of facilitated training sessions is to understand the business as a whole, but it also allows each team member to learn the step-by-step process involved in the jobs they are hired for. It is the main training tool for the franchisee's staff. Most importantly, the Ops Manual is your quality control tool.

Every single step in the development and operation of the franchisee's new business is documented, starting with the three basics:

- Practicalities of launch: finding a location, opening a bank account, obtaining a federal tax identification number, thinking about hiring and training staff.

- Legalities: discussions on human resources/labor issues such as wage and labor laws, EEOC, sexual harassment, the Americans with Disabilities Act, and a variety of other laws affecting small business.

- Operations: very specific instructions on the daily operations of the business, reporting requirements and expected standards of performance. Many franchisors will call this the Training Manual instead, but you must have it documented.

Your strong training program is a way to reinforce the Operations Manual, to clone the look, feel, and service of the franchisor business, and to make sure every employee knows their job and how it contributes to the business as a whole.

KEEP ON TRAINING

Don't assume that initial training — the training you give a new person on his first day or in their first week — is the only training you need to outline and offer in your program. The best, most profitable and highest top line revenue businesses in the country do continuous training throughout the year. They also continuously train all of their managers. Results can be improved by up to 30-40% when training is an ongoing part of what is expected of the manager and all staff members.

Starbucks trains their new hires for two full weeks before they are even allowed to 'get their hands on it' and make and sell a coffee. They have quarterly (according to the most recent information) late nights when all staff come in for a massive clean-up of the store, and more training is carried out. No doubt about it: Starbucks' bottom line and worldwide expansion have hugely benefited from thorough, repeated staff training.

Don't pinch pennies on training! Many companies do not consider the time that their employees are in training classes as paid work time, but you must.

Make training sessions an integral part of each employee's job description — "training sessions as assigned" — and pay them their usual hourly rate for participation.

Again, your outsourced Human Resources consultant can help you map out the exact training you need, but don't forget your own current staff. Your current staff knows exactly what it is they need to know — the skills, equipment experience, soft skills like communicating to customers, etc. — so be sure to question them when you build the training program for your franchisees.

And by the way, the franchise owner gets the same training from you that the staff will get from him or her, with the addition of reporting and other high-level management expectations and processes. Make sure there is a section in the training program for franchisees to refer to on all administrative and management issues; this should be considered absolutely essential.

Franchisee Real Estate, Purchasing & Setup

You've sold your first franchise, now what?

But you are not quite done yet. Franchise candidates will look to you for help in finding a commercial property (this calls for realtors), and working with your approved vendors on purchasing all the necessary fixtures, furniture, and equipment (this calls for build-out/remodeling project management). Once a location is secured, your franchisee will need assistance during the construction phase to know how much that will cost them, what to expect, and how long things should take.

Who is going to help your franchisee find their real estate, secure financing, handle construction, set up with all the vendors, handle the grand opening, launch their website, do marketing set-ups, and recruit/hire staff...? You need to be prepared and have the properly skilled in-house or outsourced team in place to ensure that you can handle all of these issues.

These are all questions that can help create a scary time for a new franchisor. So let's think through all of these items so that you are able to assist your franchisees like a pro through the ins and outs of their launch (which you should look at as your launch too).

FRANCHISEE REAL ESTATE

How much help and support can you provide to franchisees with their real estate selection? As the franchisor, the franchisee will be looking to you for guidance on what locations are best and why. If you do not have real estate experience, we strongly suggest using a franchise-friendly commercial realtor or outsourcing your franchise real estate to a company that specializes in just that process (they do exist).

FRANCHISEE PURCHASING PROGRAM

One of the main reasons people buy a franchise is so they do not have to figure everything out on their own. We recommend putting together a purchasing program — and another manual — to make your franchise as turnkey as possible. Say your business has eight vendors and $100,000 worth of equipment that needs to be purchased. Instead of giving your franchisee a list of eight vendors for them to contact and negotiate with, simply sell them a turnkey package that includes everything they need in one simple package. Basically, you can be the middleman and make it easy for your franchisees (and perhaps make yourself a bit more money in the process).

FRANCHISEE SET-UP

In addition to the training, the franchisee is going to expect someone to come and actually help them launch and set up the store so it is correctly 'Opening Day ready'. Again, this could be a 2-3 day visit to help them get everything up and running, but planning accordingly is invaluable. In addition to having a two-week training program where franchisees can be grouped together, you will also need to provide set-up support as well. This, however, for obvious reasons, cannot be combined. Those trips and your staffing need to be planned wisely.

Franchisee Ongoing Support & Training

You have now sold your first franchise and helped your first franchisee understand many of the issues involved in getting to Opening Day. Now you have the exciting and challenging role of helping that new franchisee make a go of their business.

If you are a retail business, it is no secret: there are a lot of things that need to happen before that franchisee is able to open his or her business and start making money. We strongly suggest you have a checklist of items prepared to assist the franchisee with accomplishing everything they need to do to get the process started.

We call this process *Franchisee Onboarding*, which is essentially the time between when they pay the franchise fee and sign the agreement, and when they come to training. We highly recommend in a retail environment that franchisees have already found a location and signed a lease for it before coming to training school, as it could take (in some cases) months to secure a location. Why? If a franchisee attends training the week after signing and does not find a location for 90 days and then it takes another 90 days to build out, they could be six months out of training and may not remember anything they were taught.

It is vital to have a well thought out onboarding process for your franchisees and your corporate staff to follow.

ONGOING FRANCHISEE SUPPORT

For your established franchisees only, I strongly suggest setting up a digital/phone support ticket system like www.FreshDesk.com very early on to help you monitor and track franchisee support requests to you and your team. It is important that someone is there to respond immediately to calls and/or emails from franchisees.

Keep in mind many franchisees are investing their life savings and have been part of corporate America their whole lives. So being a business owner might well be brand new to them, and things that are normal as a business owner to you may be foreign to them. Your best bet is to be available, patient, and understanding of each franchisee's unique needs. If you have done everything right, by several months after their Opening Day, they will be functioning on their own with ease.

If you see your candidate is becoming a mistake or is in any way not cut out for business ownership (or just *this* business ownership) in the long-term, refer back to the franchise resale section and have a talk with the individual.

Conclusion

I've consulted with owners who have followed the analysis process to the point of determining that their current business is franchise-eligible according to the guidelines I've presented. Then I see the real worry begin in them because it can indeed seem like a daunting process to complete. But there is no need for worry! When you have taken the strategic decision of becoming a franchisor, there is lots of professional help to get you to launch day and even guide you through the first few franchisee launches.

I have also consulted with a handful of people without any business experience at all, but they know upfront they want to become a franchisor. How can they do this without a business to franchise? This seems odd but is not: they are simply in search-mode. They are searching for the right brand-new business concept with potential; they will then start that brand-new business from scratch, with franchising it as their chosen strategy for growth firmly in mind.

That is indeed an advantage! They map out the details before launching the startup business; they fine tune operational processes for a year or so and document everything; they develop a great repeat customer base, ongoing staff training, and a profit-making marketing and sales plan. When they go live with their franchise, much of the work is already produced, tried, and tested. While it is true that no brand-new business concept is guaranteed to succeed and prosper, it is a smart wealth-building strategy resulting from big upfront efforts with the initial business, and franchisees who take it from there.

If you still have doubts or questions, please realize this: your current single-location or multi-location business does not have to be large in terms of number of employees. It doesn't have to be worth any certain 'standard' amount in top-line revenues or have a market valuation of any predetermined amount.

What does it need? Your business does need to be consistently profitable. It does need to be replicable or 'cloneable' by a franchisee. You may not have all the typical franchise-required processes and procedures in place or documented, but just know that, with support and clear thinking, you will reach that state where you possess full and detailed Operations Manuals and have your approved, filed FDD and FA.

Should you need further advice beyond what I have presented in these pages, call me for a consultation. I can be reached here:
www.HowToFranchiseBook.com

Resources and References

TOP 20 FRANCHISING STORIES

Here are my Top 20 All-Time Great Franchise Stories. You'll recognize most of the names, so why not read the stories of those franchisors that are unfamiliar to you?

1) **KFC Founder Colonel Harland Sanders**
   https://www.biography.com/business-figure/colonel-harland-sanders

   https://bit.ly/3fBS2bT

2) **Billionaire Subway founder Fred Deluca**
   https://www.entrepreneur.com/article/313130

   https://bit.ly/398rVXU

3) **Billionaire Jimmy Johns Founder Jimmy John Liautaud**
   https://www.forbes.com/sites/noahkirsch/2019/01/02/when-a-billionaire-needs-a-boss-the-story-of-the-jimmy-johns-sandwich-empire/#49df7425540c

   https://bit.ly/32rQrBK

4) **Wendy's founder Dave Thomas**
   https://www.biography.com/business-figure/dave-thomas

   https://bit.ly/2Oubxau

5) **Ray Kroc from McDonald's**
   https://www.biography.com/business-figure/ray-kroc

   https://bit.ly/2CEfpDc

6) **Billionaire Michael Ilitch from Little Caesars Pizza**
   https://littlecaesars.com/en-us/our-history/

   https://bit.ly/3967jiS

7) **Billionaire WW2 Vet Jack C. Taylor from Enterprise Rental Car**
   https://www.enterpriseholdings.com/en/press-archive/2016/07/jack-crawford-taylor-war-hero-business-leader-philanthropist.html

   https://bit.ly/3j7SAZv

8) **Billionaire William Barron Hilton from Hilton Hotels**
   https://biography.yourdictionary.com/barron-hilton

   https://bit.ly/394vMVB

9) **Billionaire JW Marriot from Marriot Hotels**
   https://www.marriott.com/culture-and-values/marriott-family-history.mi

   https://bit.ly/3hcpA0z

10) **Joe C. Thompson from 7/11**
    https://www.britannica.com/topic/7-Eleven

    https://bit.ly/2CCZ5m9

11) **Ace Hardware Founders**
http://www.fundinguniverse.com/company-histories/
ace-hardware-corporation-history/

https://bit.ly/2ZA1PJV

12) **Jani King Founder Jim Cavanaugh**
https://www.encyclopedia.com/reference/
dictionaries-thesauruses-pictures-and-press-releases/
jani-king-international-inc

https://bit.ly/2DIOS8a

13) **Kumon Math & Reading franchise Founder
Toru Kumon from Japan**
https://www.kumon.com/about-kumon/history

https://bit.ly/2CLysf2

14) **Baskin Robbins Story**
https://www.mashed.com/177683/the-untold-truth-of-
baskin-robbins/

https://bit.ly/396FLtv

15) **Great Clips Story**
https://www.greatclipsfranchise.com/the-great-clips-advantage/
brand-and-history/a-great-story-our-history

https://bit.ly/3fDK42b

16) **Budget Blinds Story**
https://www.forbes.com/sites/karstenstrauss/2019/04/16/
how-five-guys-from-california-laid-the-founda
tion-for-a-670m-home-improvement-business/#212f3e855e02

https://bit.ly/3h5FASb

17) **Five Guys Burger Story**
https://www.fiveguys.com/fans/the-five-guys-story

https://bit.ly/3fC0yYH

18) **Anytime Fitness Story**
https://www.entrepreneur.com/article/315140

https://bit.ly/3fHl0qY

19) **Orange Theory Fitness Story**
https://www.fastcompany.com/90201967/how-orangetheory-grew-to-dominate-the-boutique-fitness-industry

https://bit.ly/30J7cWC

20) **Goldfish Swim School**
https://www.goldfishswimschool.com/about/our-story/

https://bit.ly/32uXlGr

GREAT BOOKS ON FRANCHISING

- *Franchise Your Business* by Mark Siebert

- *So You Want to Franchise Your Business* by Harold Kestenbaum

- *The e-Myth Revisited* by Michael Gerber

- *The Franchise MBA* by Nick Neonakis

- *Franchising for Dummies* by Michael H. Seid & Dave Thomas

- *The Educated Franchisee: Find the Right Franchise for You*, 3rd Edition by Rick Bisio

- *Grow Smart, Risk Less: A Low-Capital Path to Multiplying Your Business Through Franchising* by Shelly Sun

HOW TO FIND FDDs ONLINE

There are four states that publish FDDs online, but only the brands registered in that specific state will be listed on these websites. So, if you're looking for a company that only has Texas locations, the franchise disclosure document will not be listed on these websites.

- **California**
  https://docqnet.dbo.ca.gov/search

  https://bit.ly/2XxPAMH

- **Indiana**
  https://securities.sos.in.gov/public-portfolio-search

  https://bit.ly/2DCeyDC

- **Minnesota**
  https://www.cards.commerce.state.mn.us/CARDS/view/index.xhtml

  https://bit.ly/3i4kKmK

- **Wisconsin**
  https://www.wdfi.org/apps/FranchiseSearch/MainSearch.aspx

  https://bit.ly/33u9o7n

If you cannot find the FDDs on these free searches, you can attempt to contact the franchisor directly and ask for it, or mystery shop their franchise sales department. If you don't want to creep around to get the FDDs, you can also use paid services like the following:

- https://fddexchange.com

- https://www.frandata.com/products-solutions/fdds-franchise-disclosure-documents

  https://bit.ly/2DGdUVK

TOP GENERAL FRANCHISING WEBSITES

- **The Franchise Rule Compliance Guide can be found here:**
  https://www.ftc.gov/system/files/documents/plain-language/bus70-franchise-rule-compliance-guide.pdf

  https://bit.ly/3jdP939

- **Entrepreneur Franchise 500**
  https://www.entrepreneur.com/franchise500/2020

- **International Franchise Association**
  https://www.franchise.org/

- **1851 Franchise**
  https://1851franchise.com/

- **Franchise Business Review**
  https://franchisebusinessreview.com/

- **Franchise Times**
  https://www.franchisetimes.com/

- **FranData**
  https://www.frandata.com/

- **Franchise Wizards blog**
  (https://franchisewizardsblog.com/2017/05/19/franchise-arrangement-types/)

  https://bit.ly/2WRiDud

TOP FRANCHISE TRADESHOWS

- **International Franchise Expo**
  https://www.ifeinfo.com/

- **The Franchise Expo**
  http://www.franchiseshowinfo.com/

TOP FRANCHISOR WEBSITE, SOCIAL, MARKETING & PR AGENCIES

- **Scorpion**
  https://www.scorpion.co/

- **Integrated Digital Strategies**
  https://www.idigitalstrategies.com/

- **ClickTecs**
  https://clicktecs.com/

- **Curious Jane**
  https://curiousjane.com/

- **Rev Local**
  https://www.revlocal.com/

- **Meet Soci**
  https://www.meetsoci.com/

- **Fishman PR**
  https://www.fishmanpr.com/

- **Wheat Creative**
  https://wheatcreative.com/

- **All Points PR**
  http://allpointspr.com/

- **Fish PR**
  https://fish-consulting.com/

- **Franchise Elevator**
  http://franchiseelevator.com/

- **No Limit Agency**
  https://www.nolimitagency.com/

TOP FRANCHISE ATTORNEYS

- **Internicola Law Firm**
  https://www.franchiselawsolutions.com/

- **DLA Piper**
  https://www.dlapiper.com/

- **Greenberg Traurig**
  https://www.gtlaw.com/en/capabilities/franchise--distribution

- **Fisher Zucker**
  https://fisherzucker.com/

- **Cheng Cohen**
  https://www.chengcohen.com/

FRANCHISE ATTORNEYS AND THE FRANCHISE RULE

- http://watkinslawfirm.com/index.php/blog/item/53-what-is-the-franchise-rule-and-what-should-i-know-about-franchising

  https://bit.ly/39g5Rux

- https://www.ftc.gov/enforcement/rules/rulemaking-regulatory-reform-proceedings/franchise-rule

  https://bit.ly/2WJtJld

- https://www.ftc.gov/tips-advice/business-center/guidance/franchise-rule-compliance-guide

  https://bit.ly/3fFFAYW

- https://www.ftc.gov/tips-advice/business-center/guidance/amended-franchise-rule-faqs

  https://bit.ly/2Zz0I2O

TOP FRANCHISE SALES LEAD PORTALS & GENERATORS

- **Entrepreneur.com**
  https://entrepreneurmedia.com/

- **Franchise Help**
  https://www.franchisehelp.com/

- **Franchise Direct**
  https://www.franchisedirect.com/

- **5th Avenue Lead**
  https://5thavenueleads.com/

- **Exec Leads**
  http://www.execleads.com/

OTHER GREAT RESOURCES

Selling your franchise opportunity is always about having an edge and continuously honing your knowledge and presentation skills. Some great resources for understanding the psychology and tools behind franchise sales are:

- https://educatedfranchisee.com/

- *"Franchisor Guide to Common Mistakes in Selling Franchises"*, by Kara Martin, available at: http://www.franchisebusinesslawgroup. com/franchisor-guide-to-common-mistakes-in-selling-franchises-2/

  https://bit.ly/3fWm62i

TOP FRANCHISE BROKER COMPANIES

- **Transworld Business Advisors**
  https://www.tworld.com/

- **International Franchise Professionals group (IFPG)**
  https://www.ifpg.org/

- **Franchise Brokers Association**
  https://www.franchiseba.com/

- **FranNet**
  https://frannet.com/

TOP FRANCHISE FINANCE COMPANIES

- **FranFund**
  https://www.franfund.com/

- **Boefly**
  http://www.boefly.com/

- **Guidant Financial**
  https://www.guidantfinancial.com/

- **Benetrends**
  https://www.benetrends.com/

TOP FRANCHISOR SAAS/SOFTWARE

- **FranConnect**
  https://www.franconnect.com/

- **Naranga**
  https://naranga.com/

- **FRM Solutions**
  https://www.frmsolutions.com/

- **QuickBooks Franchisor**
  https://quickbooks.intuit.com/franchise/

- **Constant Contact Franchisor**
  https://www.constantcontact.com/partners/franchise

TOP FRANCHISE SALES OUTSOURCING COMPANIES

- **Accurate Franchising**
  https://www.accuratefranchising.com/

- **Franchise Performance Group**
  https://franchiseperformancegroup.com/

- **Raintree Sales**
  https://raintreesales.com/

Get the most out of your franchising journey

This book comes with a companion workbook, videos, and additional resources. All are available at

www.HowToFranchiseBook.com

 **JASON R. ANDERSON, MBA** is a franchising expert, speaker, consultant, author, and college level instructor. While serving in the United States Air Force (active duty on 9/11), Jason started his first business. At only 23 years old, Jason sold that business, moved to Dallas, and got started in real estate in 2007. By 2011, his company had nearly 200 agents, three offices, and was the 8th largest real estate company by transaction volume in the State of Texas. Jason knew he had better systems, marketing programs, and service offerings than his largest competitors, RE/MAX and Keller Williams, and he couldn't figure out how they had 100,000 agents compared to his 200 (500x more). Then he realized what they both had in common: They were both franchise opportunities. This is how Jason got his start in the franchising world. He subsequently sold his real estate business to a publicly traded company and was honored as recipient of *Forbes* 30 Under 30. He was featured on the cover of *Realtor Magazine*, received the *Dallas Business Journal* Minority Business Leader Award, and appeared on TLC's *My First Home*. Today, Jason lives in Dallas with his wife, Claire, daughter, Ella Grace, and their two dogs. He sits on the board of United Franchise Group and is the president of Venture X, the fastest growing flexible office space franchise in the world, overseeing its growth to 32 locations open and 125 sold in 31 countries in only 4 years.

WHAT CLIENTS AND COLLEAGUES SAY ABOUT JASON

"It is rare to work with a genuine talent such as Jason. We worked together for five years at United Franchise Group growing the Transworld Business Advisors brand and again in developing a successful national franchisor resale program. I was awestruck by Jason's seemingly effortless ability to quickly create new and innovative solutions to any challenge. No matter what the situation, Jason had a creative idea for moving forward in the most productive manner. I can confidently recommend Jason for any undertaking he chooses to pursue."

—Jeff Griffith, CBI, CFC, Director of Franchise Sales and Development
at Jackson Hewitt Tax Service Inc.

"Jason is a cornucopia of knowledge and the epitome of execution. He knows how to get things done!"

—Jaffar Wahdat, Founder and CEO

"It is truly a pleasure working with Jason. In every interaction we've had, he's consistently professional, responsive, and helpful. Further, His knowledge and understanding of franchise development is incredibly impressive. Can't recommend him enough!"

—Andrea Thieman, Planning Analyst at Allegheny County
Department of Human Services

"Having worked with hundreds of franchise development professionals across the industry, I am confident that there are few other at Jason's level. His understanding of what it takes to be successful and most important commitment to executing on that plan is unrivaled. As technology continues to influence the franchising community, there may be no one better positioned for the future. Anyone with the chance to work with him is truly lucky!"

—Eli Robinson, COO at Metric Collective

"I've had the great pleasure of working with Jason Anderson since early 2015. We worked hand-in-hand on building a robust franchise development digital marketing program for all UFG brands as well as "AFI" — the franchise consulting arm to UFG. In that time, I've learned so much from who I refer to as "one of the brightest minds in franchise development marketing" Jason Anderson. He has a vast understanding on how to maximize franchise lead generation and building efficiencies & measurability better than any client I've every worked with. Not to mention, he is always looking at ways to gain an edge in this very competitive industry. Needless to say, Jason is a winner in every sense of the word. My organization has the utmost respect and admiration for him and everything he is about."

—Joseph A. Mohay, MBA, Chief Revenue Officer and Co-Founder, Franchise Marketing Strategist, 20 Year Digital Marketing Veteran

"I've had a great experience working with Jason. He's been professional, responsive and helpful. His knowledge of the franchise industry is extensive. Our strategic planning session was invaluable. I highly recommend him."

—Steven Schaef, Director of Operations at Urban Mattress

"Jason and I have worked together over the past year on many different projects across multiple UFG brands. He has always been a pleasure to work with and he brings a lot to the table with his great knowledge of the franchise industry. I'm always impressed with his ability to bring new ideas to our discussions and keep franchise initiatives current and cutting edge. He's quick, responsive, and works diligently to meet his goals with the company's best interest at heart."

—Madeline Ta'ala, Digital Marketing Manager

"I have had the pleasure of working with Jason during his time at United Franchise Group when he managed Franchise Development, and now as President of Accurate Franchising, Inc. Throughout my tenure working with Jason, I have found him to be one of the brightest, up and coming, young professionals in the franchising industry. Jason combines the rare ability to understand the big picture, while at the same time having a complete under-standing of the details that are so important when managing critical aspects of a company with several million dollars in revenue. Jason is aways interested in the latest trends in digital marketing and ready to take advantage of new ideas to help him expand the rapid growth that the United Franchise Group enjoys. Most importantly, Jason is great guy who garners the respect of those around him and is a pleasure to work with!"

—Stephen Galligan, CEO

"Since I started working with United Franchise Group (UFG) and Accurate Franchising Inc (AFI) in 2010, Transworld Business Advisors has exploded across the world. We have over 100 offices in the USA and now in several countries. There is no doubt, my company could never have achieved those results without the expertise and amazing work by UFG/AFI. Franchising my business was a goal of mine, but after looking into the process, we decided not to move forward. Until I met the folks at UFG and saw firsthand their capa-bilities at their West Palm Beach headquarters. I was sold and thankfully made the decision to partner with them. If you intend to franchise your business or need to expand your current franchise. Look no further than the professionals at AFI and UFG."

—Andrew Cagnetta, Founder, Transworld Business Advisors

Made in the USA
Middletown, DE
01 July 2021

43417972R00086